Publishing Pedagogies for th Doctorate and Beyond

Within a context of rapid growth and diversification in higher degree research programmes, there is increasing pressure for the results of doctoral research to be made public. Doctoral students are now being encouraged to publish not only after completion of the doctorate, but also during, and even as part of their research programme. For many this is a new and challenging feature of their experience of doctoral education.

Publishing Pedagogies for the Doctorate and Beyond is a timely and informative collection of practical and theorized examples of innovative pedagogies that encourage doctoral student publishing. The authors give detailed accounts of their own pedagogical practices so that others may build on their experiences, including: a programme of doctoral degree by publication; mentoring strategies to support student publishing; innovations within existing programmes, including embedded publication pedagogies; co-editing a special issue of a scholarly journal with students; 'publication brokering'; and writing groups and writing retreats.

With contributions from global leading experts, this vital new book:

- explores broader issues pertaining to journal publication and the impacts on scholarly research and writing practices for students, supervisors and the academic publishing community;
- takes up particular pedagogical problems and strategies, including curriculum and supervisory responses arising from the 'push to publish';
- documents explicit experiences and practical strategies that foster writing-for-publication during doctoral candidature.

Publishing Pedagogies for the Doctorate and Beyond explores the challenges and rewards of supporting doctoral publishing and provides new ways to increase research publication outputs in a pedagogically sound way. It will be a valued resource for supervisors and their doctoral students, as well as for programme coordinators and managers, academic developers, learning advisors and others involved in doctoral education.

Claire Aitchison is Senior Lecturer in Postgraduate Literacies at the University of Western Sydney, Australia.

Barbara Kamler is Emeritus Professor of Education at Deakin University, Australia.

Alison Lee is Professor of Education at the University of Technology, Sydney, Australia.

Publishing Pedagogies for the Doctorate and Beyond

Edited by Claire Aitchison,
Barbara Kamler and Alison Lee

Routledge
Taylor & Francis Group

LONDON AND NEW YORK

First published 2010
by Routledge
2 Park Square, Milton Park, Abingdon, Oxon, OX14 4RN

Simultaneously published in the USA and Canada
by Routledge
270 Madison Avenue, New York, NY 10016

Routledge is an imprint of the Taylor & Francis Group, an informa business

Typeset in Garamond by Prepress Projects Ltd, Perth, UK
Printed and bound in Great Britain by MPG Books Group

British Library Cataloguing in Publication Data
A catalogue record for this book is available from the British Library

Library of Congress Cataloging-in-Publication Data
Publishing pedagogies for the doctorate and beyond / edited by Claire
Aitchison, Barbara Kamler, and Alison Lee.
p. cm.
1. Scholarly publishing. 2. Academic writing—Study and teaching (Graduate)
3. Dissertations, Academic. 4. Universities and colleges—Graduate work. I.
Aitchison, Claire. II. Kamler, Barbara. III. Lee, Alison, 1952–
Z286.S37P83 2010
070.5—dc22
2009029263

ISBN10: 0–415–48018–3 (hbk)
ISBN10: 0–415–48019–1 (pbk)
ISBN10: 0–203–86096–9 (ebk)

ISBN13: 978–0–415–48018–5 (hbk)
ISBN13: 978–0–415–48019–2 (pbk)
ISBN13: 978–0–203–86096–0 (ebk)

Contents

Illustrations

Figures

Tables

Contributors

Claire Aitchison is Senior Lecturer with special responsibilities for graduate student literacies at the University of Western Sydney. She has 17 years' experience developing innovative practical pedagogies for supporting academic writing across a broad range of disciplines and research areas. In recent years she has developed, researched and taught writing programmes for doctoral students, early career researchers and academic staff. Claire's teaching and curriculum design are noted for their incorporation of peer learning through the pedagogy of peer review. She has written widely on the efficacy of writing groups for doctoral education.

Richard Beach is Professor of English Education at the University of Minnesota. He is author or co-author of *Teaching Writing Using Blogs, Wikis, and Other Digital Tools* (Christopher-Gordon, 2008); *Teaching Literature to Adolescents* (Routledge, 2006); *Teachingmedialiteracy.com: A Web-based Guide to Links and Activities* (Teachers College Press, 2006); and *High School Students' Competing Social Worlds: Negotiating Identities and Allegiances through Responding to Multicultural Literature* (Routledge, 2007). He is also the organizing editor for the annual Annotated Bibliography of Research for *Research in the Teaching of English* and is a member of the NCTE Commission on Media.

Tina Byrom is Lecturer in Educational Development at Nottingham Trent University and contributes to the undergraduate joint honours programme. She completed her PhD, 'The Dream of Social Flying: Social Class, Higher Education Choice and the Paradox of Widening Participation', at the University of Nottingham. Tina has significant experience of teaching in secondary schools and has worked on numerous research projects including Understanding Teenage Pregnancy in Nottingham; Health Imperatives in Schools; HE Participation Rates in Nottingham North; and FE Provision in Nottingham City. Her research interests include issues of social justice and inclusion, pupil voice and the educational experiences of young people.

Christine Pearson Casanave lived in Japan for over 15 years, mostly working at Keio University's Shonan Fujisawa Campus, and has also worked as adjunct at Teachers College Columbia University and Visiting Professor and adjunct at Temple University. She has a special fondness for writing (reflective and essay writing, academic writing, writing for publication), for professional development of language teachers, and for narrative, case study and qualitative inquiry. One of her long-term goals is to help expand the accepted styles of writing in the TESOL field, and another is to argue for more humanistic, less technology-driven second language education.

Barbara Kamler is Emeritus Professor at Deakin University, Melbourne, and Honorary Professor at the University of Sydney. Her research on the social practices of writing have traversed the lifespan, from early childhood to old age, in primary, secondary, university and community education contexts. Her most recent work focuses on doctoral writing and publication and she currently runs workshops in Australia and internationally to help early career academics develop authoritative writing and a robust publication record. Recent book publications include *Relocating the Personal: A Critical Writing Pedagogy* (SUNY, 2001) and *Helping Doctoral Students Write: Pedagogies for Supervision* (with Pat Thomson, Routledge, 2006).

Alison Lee is Professor of Education and Director of the Centre for Research in Learning and Change at UTS. She has researched and published extensively in higher and professional education, with a particular focus on doctoral education, including doctoral writing, doctoral supervision, professional doctorates, and the changing relations between the university and the professions. Her co-edited book with David Boud, *Changing Practice of Doctoral Education* (Routledge, 2009), addresses the globalization of the doctorate, including implications for doctoral writing and publication.

Rowena Murray worked in the Centre for Academic Practice at Strathclyde University for 15 years and is now Reader and Associate Dean (Research) in the Education Faculty. She supervises PhD students and runs workshops, courses and consultancies on academic writing. Her research has been funded by the British Academy and the Nuffield Foundation. She publishes books and articles on academic writing, including *How to Write a Thesis* (Open University Press, 2006) and *Writing for Academic Journals* (Open University Press, 2009). She is editor of a series on higher education, beginning with *The Scholarship of Teaching and Learning in Higher Education* (Open University Press, 2009), and co-author (with Adrian Eley) of *How to be an Effective Supervisor* (Open University Press, 2009).

Anthony Paré is Professor in the Department of Integrated Studies in Education at McGill University, editor of the *McGill Journal of Education*, and former Director of the Centre for the Study and Teaching of Writing.

His research examines academic and non-academic writing, workplace learning, school-to-work transitions, and the development of professional literacies. He teaches courses in literacy, language across the curriculum, and writing theory, research and practice. His publications include books, chapters and articles on topics related to the study and practice of professional communication.

Carol Robinson is Senior Research Fellow at the University of Brighton. Her research interests focus around student voice, the transfer/development of good practice within and between schools, and the professional development of teachers. She has led a number of pupil voice projects in primary and secondary schools, helping staff develop ways of listening to the young people they work with. Carol led the 'Pupils' Voices' strand of the University of Cambridge Primary Review of Education in England and is currently working with UNICEF to evaluate its school-based Rights, Respecting Schools Programme. She is an experienced teacher who has taught in secondary schools and pupil referral units.

Lisa Russell is Senior Research Fellow at the University of Huddersfield in the Centre for Research in Post-Compulsory Education. She gained a PhD on 'Pupil Resistance to Their Schooling Experience' and a first class combined honours degree in social studies and psychology at Aston University before becoming a Research Fellow in the School of Education at the University of Nottingham. She has published in the areas of ethnography, mentoring and disaffected youth. Her research interests include issues of social justice, pupil voice and young people's experiences of inclusion and exclusion.

Amanda Haertling Thein is Assistant Professor of English Education at the University of Pittsburgh, where she studies socio-cultural aspects of response to literature and multicultural literature instruction. Dr Thein is co-author of *High School Students' Competing Social Worlds: Negotiating Identities and Allegiances through Responding to Multicultural Literature* (Routledge, 2007) and was a 2007 recipient of the National Council of Teachers of English Promising Researcher Award.

Pat Thomson is Professor of Education and Director of Research in the School of Education, the University of Nottingham. A former head teacher in disadvantaged schools, her research focuses on head teachers' work, school change, the arts and creativity, the education of marginalized children and young people, and doctoral education and writing. She is an editor of the Taylor & Francis international peer-refereed journal, *Educational Action Research*. Recent publications include *Helping Doctoral Students Write: Pedagogies for Supervision* (with Barbara Kamler, Routledge, 2006), *Doing Visual Research with Children and Young People* (Routledge, 2008) and *School Leadership – Heads on the Block?* (Routledge, 2009).

Chapter 1

Introduction

Why publishing pedagogies?

Claire Aitchison, Barbara Kamler and Alison Lee

The pressure to publish

It is an exciting time to be involved in doctoral education. There is an explosion of interest and innovation in higher degree research processes and practices, as universities seek to respond to local, national and international changes. In an increasingly competitive global economy, universities have been required to show greater accountability as governments and industry expect a good return for their investment: a more rapid and public dissemination of research results and the delivery of employment-ready graduates (Boud and Lee, 2009).

Within this context, earlier notions of what count as knowledge, research and 'research training' are being questioned and contested. As regional and national governments reassess research and higher education in the context of broader economic, social and environmental forces, there have been a range of responses. In Europe, we have seen the third cycle of the Bologna Process and the establishment of the Council for Doctoral Education (see www.eua. be); in the UK, the *Report on the Review of Research Degree Programmes: England and Northern Ireland* (QAA, 2007); in the USA, the Woodrow Wilson Foundation *Responsive PhD Project* (2000) and the *Carnegie Initiative on the Doctorate* (Carnegie Foundation, 2002); and in Australia, most recently, an *Inquiry into Research Training and Research Workforce Issues in Australian Universities* (Department of Education, Employment and Workplace Relations, 2008). At the same time, the doctorate has come under the direct influence of regulatory regimes for the management of quality – for example the UK Quality Assurance Agency for Higher Education and the Australian Universities Quality Agency. Within the context of this increased scrutiny of doctoral education, areas of tension have been identified concerning high attrition and low completion rates (Golde and Walker, 2006) and debates have intensified about the quality of training for doctoral degrees and the competency of graduates (e.g. Park, 2007).

One result is broader recognition of the need for re-envisaging approaches to the education of research students (Boud and Lee, 2009). As Bitusikova (2009) notes, for example, a key question in all of the current debates about doctoral education across Europe centres on the choice of the most appropriate organizational structures. In policy terms, structures must 'demonstrate added value for the institution and for doctoral candidates: to improve transparency, quality, and admission and assessment procedures; and to create synergies regarding transferable skills development' (Bitusikova, 2009: 202–3). Traditionally conceived individual study programmes based on an implicit model of a 'working alliance between the doctoral candidate and the supervisor without a structured coursework phase' are being increasingly critiqued as being 'inappropriate to meet challenges of training for multiple careers in a global labour market' (ibid.: 203).

Such developments mean that the experience of doctoral study for students and for supervisors is changing. Students are increasingly expected to complete their studies in a shorter time frame and be more 'productive' during the period of their enrolment (Lee and Aitchison, 2009). This demand for greater 'productivity' finds most direct expression in the push to publish their research (McGrail, Rickard and Jones, 2006; Lee and Kamler, 2008; Hartley and Betts, 2009). Increasingly these developments take place on an international stage, in an era of advanced communication technologies and international university league tables (Nerad, 2006; Bell, Hill and Leaming, 2007). Indeed, it could be argued that the intensity of global competition among universities and national systems, together with attempts to measure the quality of research through publications data and doctoral completions in addition to research income, has distorted the space in which doctoral work is done and research careers are forged.

Clearly, major questions arise about the implications of such shifts for our research programmes and courses. How are individual research students, their supervisors and institutions responding? What kinds of skills, attributes and competencies are required of doctoral students and those who work with them, in order to provide a rich and successful experience of entering the world of scholarly peer review and publication?

The focus of this book

In this book we explore the questions, dilemmas and responses to the increasing expectation that doctoral students publish their research, both after their doctorate is complete and, more and more, it seems, along the way. We are interested in explicitly foregrounding the pedagogical practices that are at issue: what is to be learned about scholarly publication of doctoral research, and how is it to be facilitated, managed or taught? We are aware of the paucity of information about the everyday practices in the lifeworld of doctoral students and supervisors wishing to promote and develop writing for publication. And we are aware of the challenges for supervisors and universities in managing this new pressure in a principled and skilful way.

In the current climate, universities are often happy that their research students are publishing, but often not skilful in recognizing the pedagogical work involved in bringing students into a productive relationship with the practices of publication. Our emphasis, by contrast, is on doctoral pedagogies that bring writing to the fore because our own experiences as practitioners convince us how powerfully learning can occur when students are writing *as they research and learn*. We are also acutely aware of how important it is to make the pedagogical work of developing writing and building know-how about scholarly publication visible when the focus of policy makers and institutional stakeholders is solely on 'counting' student output in publication audits and the like.

At the outset of this project we shared a hunch that new relationships were starting to emerge between student research and the expanded genres employed for writing about that research. We recognized that the traditional, almost sacred, status of the 'thesis' or 'dissertation'[1] was rapidly altering, and that its prominence was being challenged. Certainly the contemporary market place, with its voracious appetite for new knowledge and new graduates, appears to be increasingly intolerant of the lengthy timeframes and the inaccessibility of the old-fashioned tome: the doctoral thesis.

As we envisaged this project, we were motivated by a desire to find out how students, their supervisors and institutions are responding to new pressures to make research public during the period of doctoral candidature. We wanted to explore in detail a relatively small number of examples of pedagogies that we knew were explicitly engaging writing for publication. And we were particularly interested in giving space to the complexities and nuances of the actual practices of teaching and learning. So this book does not pretend to be a handbook of practices or an instruction manual, and it certainly does not give an account of all that is exciting and innovative in this changing landscape of doctoral research education.

What this edited collection does do, we believe, is showcase the work of a group of dedicated academics who are exploring ways to build research cultures that incorporate and support student publishing. The stories laid out in these chapters reflect an unevenness in the development of doctoral education pedagogies – from pockets of innovation championed by individuals without strong institutional support to robust, innovative system-wide publication-focused doctoral programmes. Some writers engage in this pedagogical work because it is a normal and expected part of their work and others take it on as an extension to their supervisory role. In most cases it is clear that these pedagogical practices could not survive without extensive work carried out by (often already overworked) individuals, drawing on extensive cultural capital and pre-existing networks of scholars. What is common, despite their challenges and reservations, is the recognition of the value to research students of writing for a public audience.

This book deliberately and purposefully gives space to a select range of pedagogical practices from around the world, thus providing a record of the operations, challenges and rewards of some new practices that otherwise remain invisible. By placing pedagogy at the centre of this discussion, we are attending to the working life of academics and doctoral students in a rapidly changing context. At the same time, we are contributing to the bigger conversations about the purposes of doctoral education. What kinds of researchers and scholars are being produced in a publication-focused doctoral curriculum? What practices might be valued, emulated and disseminated? How might innovation be nurtured and made sustainable and mainstream?

The challenge of writing about pedagogy

From the outset, our goal has been to develop publishing pedagogies that move beyond 'tips and tricks' or technical elaborations of journal procedure, from the point of article submission through to final publication. As editors we have worked closely with our co-contributors to articulate what it is we do in our diverse educational sites to support early career publication. And yet the difficulty of writing about pedagogy remains.

It is difficult to be specific, to make the familiar strange enough to engage readers outside our context. Because our contributors write across diverse epistemological and geographic boundaries, we kept asking questions of their drafts – sometimes too persistently, occasionally to their annoyance. We wanted examples of pedagogy at work, rather than generalized accounts. We were hungry for narrative truth and texture, but we did not just want personal stories that could not be mined for broader principles.

We similarly struggled in writing our own chapters, even though we devised the book proposal and knew well its argument and stance. We regularly complained to one another that our drafts were banal, boring, too superficial, unable to capture the right data or telling incidents. Claire Aitchison, for example, who probably knows more than most about how to run writing groups – building intellectual rigour as well as emotional support into their fabric – struggled to make explicit what it was she did, how she modelled for students ways of reading and responding to writing-in-progress. If she 'led from behind', as she claimed, what did that mean and how might she convey this cogently?

We have no definitive answer about why the pedagogical rendering task is so hard, but we have three tentative explanations about why this might be so. The first has to do with the difficulty of writing as a cultural insider. When a terrain is so much a part of a teacher/writer's skin, it is often difficult to conceptualize what it is we do. It is equally problematic to try to extrapolate the specifics away from practice. Too often what emerges is a colourless de-contextualized list, which can be boring or too technical. It is difficult as an insider to attain sufficient distance, to see pattern, particularly in higher education, where writing about pedagogy is a fairly new and still less legitimate activity than writing about research.

Our second explanation relates to the problem of representation. For the most part, higher education practice is undocumented empirically, although this is changing slowly. There is not enough research that gives the texture, taste and smell of teaching and learning, the excitement as well as the failures. Tai Peseta (2007) develops this argument in the context of her work in academic development, in which she suggests that too many research accounts of practice have a deadening sameness that do not adequately capture its spirit and vitality:

> we have tended to report victory narratives that defend and extend our relevance as a community, rather than making public the intense difficulty of our work, as if that somehow sullies the credibility of the project with which we are engaged. We often write, too, with a worry that this difficulty speaks of self-indulgence, as if the pain and hurt we experience . . . ought not to spill over into our practices and relationships proper.
>
> (Peseta, 2007: 17)

Our third explanation concerns the cultural dominance of the 'how to' genre, a genre which is ubiquitous in modernity and rife in the doctoral education field. Too often, the dominant mode of communication mobilized by experts is a transmission pedagogy, which reduces the complexity of writing to a set of tools and techniques. Kamler and Thomson (2008) have critiqued the advice genre for the damage it does to both doctoral researchers and a field seeking to establish a theorized practice of academic writing and publishing. Despite this critique, we acknowledge the difficulty of writing outside the habituated processes of the genre. We certainly aim to achieve a respectful stance in this collection and explore new ways to interact with scholars in the making. A key strategy we use is to *lightly theorize* our pedagogical work, following Kamler and Thomson (2006). We leave plenty of room for practice, but conceptualize that practice so that it does not simply default into another book of advice. Our aim is to articulate coherent principles or strategies that others might interact with as we engage in the collective work of building publishing pedagogies.

Theoretical framings

We have adopted a broadly social, including socio-cultural and socio-discursive, theoretical framing in this book. Our starting point is a commitment to the centrality of pedagogy to the work of doctoral education. We take pedagogy both as a conceptual field, involving the relations among teaching, learning and the knowledge and practice being produced in that relationship (after Lusted, 1986; see also Lee and Green, 1997), and as a practice.

Practices involve action and interaction, with others and with objects and artefacts – physical environments, technical equipment, books and papers, digital media, etc. Practices are always directed towards particular goals and purposes and are always value-laden. They are socially formed and structured (Kemmis, 2009). So when we talk about practice, we are entering not an unproblematic space that is the opposite or obverse of theory, but rather one that is already replete with goals, values, assumptions, principles and rules, implicit and explicit, and sets of expectations about relationships and outcomes.

Thinking of pedagogy as a practice in this sense helps us to tease out the particularities of the 'rules, roles and relationships' (Schatzki, 2001) that are in play in any particular account of pedagogy. In Bernstein's (1971) terms, these rules, roles and relationships constitute the 'framing' of the pedagogical relation. Schatzki adds an affective dimension to his theorization of practice ('teleo-affective structures'). We see this played out in the following chapters, as writers come to grips with the dynamics of fear, desire, confusion, frustration, pleasure and satisfaction, on the part of students and those who are working with them in this arena of developing publication.

Each chapter in the collection takes up a particular theoretical stance to elaborate the pedagogical framing being described. These include new rhetorical theory (Paré, Murray), literacy theory (Aitchison), socio-discursive theories of writing and identity (Kamler, Thomson *et al.*, Casanave), curriculum theorizing (Lee), cultural-historical activity theory (Thein and Beach) and Vygotskian socio-cultural theory (Thomson, Byrom, Robinson and Russell). Each author draws on socially situated theories of pedagogical practice that are distinct and yet enter into productive dialogue with each other. We have found these theoretical resources critical to the task of moving beyond 'what we did' or 'what you need to do' to locating and understanding the ways in which pedagogical work produces sets of relations, capacities and practices going forward. Taken together, these contribute to the beginnings of a conceptualization of 'publishing pedagogies'.

The chapters

There are many possible ways to order the chapters in this book. We have chosen a method that highlights their pedagogical work and the contrasts between them, juxtaposing both like with like and similar with different. Because the chapters are multi-authored across nations, referencing local and national contexts, the stances taken differ.

The chapters can be read in any order or out of order – at a variety of sittings or in one go. This is the pleasure of an edited collection. Yet as editors we have debated and discussed the ordering in order to amplify the story we wish to tell about the urgent need for all academic communities in the social sciences to seriously rethink the way we treat publishing in relation to doctoral work. There is a pedagogical story to tell in and through the ordering and juxtaposition.

We start with Alison Lee's chapter to foreground unknown territory with new possibilities. Lee's chapter invites readers in the social sciences to imagine what a doctoral degree by publication might look and feel like by examining the case of PhDs by publication in Sweden. Through interview conversations with a doctoral supervisor and student, she explicates the pedagogies of working in this way – where the publication does not come after the dissertation or even alongside it, but *is* the thesis. The critical role of the seminar is examined, together with supervision strategies that address the design of research and manage the processes of responding to reviewers. Lee argues that many ventures into publication during doctoral study are inadequately supported, conceptually and substantively. She introduces the concept of the 'rhetorical curriculum' to emphasize the need for a systematic focus on writing and presenting work in progress in a staged process of making doctoral work public.

In Chapter 3, by contrast, Anthony Paré argues against premature doctoral publication and enumerates the dangers/problems this can cause. Paré writes from the perspective of a journal editor and doctoral supervisor – and he gives voice to both of these perspectives. He uses rhetorical theory to raise objections about the loss of an adequate learning space, free from the external pressures of publishing, in which students can feel their way into becoming scholars. Principally, he worries about what he sees as an increase in 'publication-related anxiety' among the doctoral students he works with. And he objects to the avalanche of 'undercooked' submissions from doctoral students that come across his editorial desk. But Paré also offers a pedagogy of publishing – embedded in the doctoral programme at his university – which could be easily modified by others serious about supporting students in the work of publishing their research.

Christine Casanave provides, in Chapter 4, a window into the lives of doctoral students working in a second or foreign language in Japan. In stark contrast to the working conditions of Paré and his young students, Casanave's students work within 'impossible circumstances' where she constructs a protected space to learn and practise publishing skills. She argues that pedagogies for the support of doctoral student publishing need to accommodate the realities of students' lives by bringing together, or 'dovetailing', competing personal, professional and student demands. The protected or intermediate pedagogical space produced through the Working Papers project enables students to write and edit together, with her support, to create edited collections of writings from their course work. This in-house strategy responds to the real constraints of these students and supervisors, making possible and do-able opportunities for learning the practices of scholarly publishing.

In a counterpoint to this, in Chapter 5, Barbara Kamler explores the crucial role of 'publication brokering' in the unprotected space of the revise and resubmit process. She argues that too often early career writers are left alone and unsupported to negotiate the complexities of reviewer and editor commentary. This is a frightening space full of silences, confusion and contradictions, in which supervisors, writing groups and other academic professionals can play a critical role in fostering publication success. Kamler, like Thomson *et al.*, mobilizes a conceptual frame of publishing as social discursive practice to think about brokering the social, political and cultural dimensions of revise and resubmit to help early career writers take effective textual action. She uses case studies and textual artefacts to explore two pedagogic strategies that aim to do this work and defuse the emotional response to receipt of reviewer comments.

Chapters 6 and 7 take us to spaces where pedagogies are distributed, geographically, socially and institutionally, through collective practices of writing in groups and at dedicated writing retreats. In Chapter 6, Claire Aitchison elaborates a pedagogy of multi-disciplinary research writing groups for doctoral students. She explores how the group functions as an interim space or 'safety zone' for students to become teachers, readers, reviewers, critics and editors, as they learn to engage with developing drafts of chapters and articles presented by their peers. These groups happen within the university as 'normal business', in the sense that they are resourced by the university as a deliberate strategy for writing development. Yet participation in these groups is still an individual choice, not mandated, not embedded as part of the formal curriculum. Aitchison elaborates the pedagogy she has developed over many years as a facilitator of these groups, drawing on data from documentary and evaluation inquiry she has conducted with students. This pedagogical work is a sustained practice that involves facilitating relationships and know-how over time that is accountable and becomes skilful.

Rowena Murray, in Chapter 7, takes us away from the university to the dedicated research writing retreat. This is a pedagogical space that aims to build rhetorical knowledge about writing for publication and give participants much-needed time away to focus on writing academic journal articles. Murray's specific focus is on the two-day structured retreat, in which writers all work in the same room and engage in regular goal-setting and discussion about writing-in-progress. In contrast to the noisy, talk-driven and unpredictable groups described in the previous chapter, Murray's writing retreats are characterized by slots of goal-driven, silent, productive writing. Like Aitchison, Murray explores the facilitator's role and outlines strategies to support student learning at writers' retreat. She argues that the power of being forced to write in a collegial atmosphere and learning textual strategies to manage writing anxieties has a significant impact on enhancing both publication know-how and success.

The two final chapters tell different stories of supporting doctoral students' engagement with the scholarly practices of their field. In Chapter 8, Amanda Thein and Richard Beach provide a rare account of the actual pedagogical practices of mentoring research students in writing for publication. They argue that successful pedagogies for doctoral publication involve more than simply providing rhetorical strategies by elaborating on their own relationship as student and mentor/supervisor. In this they pay particular attention to the processes of identity construction that accompany scholarly socialization. They draw on cultural-historical activity theory to situate the four mentoring strategies which they identify as critical in developing publishing expertise and know-how. These strategies include collaborative research and co-publishing, engaging in reciprocal review and evaluation, and facilitating Amanda's networking with scholarly communities. This is an explicit pedagogy of patronage and apprenticing, by an experienced researcher of a novice, into the practices and relationships of scholarly publication.

In the final chapter, Thomson, Byrom, Robinson and Russell explore the power of working together to co-edit a special issue of a peer-reviewed journal. The experience itself was mediated and made possible by Thomson's professional networks and access to research funding to support early career researchers to learn about journal editing, a neglected aspect of the publishing game. The narrative they write is multi-vocal, to make prominent their various perspectives on this collaboration. As senior member and initiator of the collaboration, Thomson explores the pedagogic work involved in *not* taking up the apprenticeship model so dominant in doctoral education. She uses Vygotsky's zone of proximal development (ZPD) to think about how the editorial tasks create a context for collective learning. She also does some preliminary thinking about how one might further scaffold the learning to edit process by treating editing as a social discursive practice that involves philosophical work, market work, profile work, relational work, textual work and secretarial work.

Taken together, the chapters in this collection illustrate a rich array of responses to the increasing pressure to publish within and beyond the doctorate. It is clear that many doctoral students, and the academics who work with them, have taken up the challenge to enter the arena of scholarly publishing with enthusiasm and determination. What the array of pedagogical practices in this book reveal is that change is happening, whether we like it or not. There is still a great deal to explore in facilitating experiences that help doctoral students develop the knowledge, skill and confidence required for success in the scholarly publishing game.

There are many indicators in the pages of this book of ways in which this pedagogical field can be opened up further to a set of new possibilities. For example, the use of digital technologies for building trans-national networks of doctoral students enabled the writing of Anna's story in Chapter 2. With shared-space real-time technologies for talking and working together on text, there are new possibilities for collaboration in scholarly writing and publishing. In addition, there are possibilities for building pedagogies that better support doctoral students in systems or disciplines that are sometimes at the periphery of the main game of scholarly publication. In an academic publishing world dominated by English, these include doctoral students who are native speakers of other languages, and particularly students in the developing world, with limited resources or access to networks of scholarly peers. Pedagogies such as that described by Casanave show us ways of working responsively within local parameters.

Much of the pedagogical work descibed in these chapters is small-scale – the work of skilled enthusiasts, working intensively with small numbers of students – in publication brokering (Kamler), in supervisor–student co-researching and co-authoring (Thein and Beach), in group work (Aitchison, Casanave, Murray, Thomson, Byron, Robinson and Russell) or in seminars (Lee, Paré). How might these pedagogies become more embedded in the 'normal business' of doctoral programmes? How can supervisors become more active and skilled in supporting appropriate and helpful publishing practices for the doctoral stiudents and graduates they work with? These questions concern the sustainability of the kinds of pedagogical initiatives described in the chapters of this book. We hope they inform debate in this growing arena.

Note

1 The terms 'thesis' and 'dissertation' are used interchangeably throughout this book to refer to the major, examinable text that describes the doctoral research.

References

Bell, R. K., Hill, D. and Lehming, R. F. (2007) *The Changing Research and Publication Environment in American Research Universities,* Working Paper SRS 07-204. Arlington, VA: Division of Science Resources Statistics, National Science Foundation, http://www.nsf.gov/statistics/srs09204/ (accessed 22 June 2009).

Bernstein, B. (1971) 'On the Classification and Framing of Educational Knowledge', in M. F. D. Young (ed.) *Knowledge and Control: New Directions for the Sociology of Education,* London: Collier Macmillan, pp. 47–69.

Bitusikova, S. (2009) 'New Challenges in Doctoral Education in Europe', in D. Boud and A. Lee (eds) *Changing Practices of Doctoral Education*, London: Routledge, pp. 200–10.

Boud, D. and Lee, A. (2009) *Changing Practices of Doctoral Education*, London: Routledge.

Carnegie Foundation for the Advancement of Teaching (2002) *Carnegie Initiative on the Doctorate*, http://www.carnegiefoundation.org/programs/ (accessed 12 June 2009).

Department of Education, Employment and Workplace Relations, Australia (2008) *Inquiry into Research Training and Research Workforce Issues in Australian Univer-*

sities, http://www.aph.gov.au/house/committee/isi/research/report.htm (accessed 23 June 2009).

Golde, C. and Walker, G. (eds, 2006) *Envisioning the Future of Doctoral Education: Preparing Stewards of the Discipline – Carnegie Essays on the Doctorate*, San Francisco, CA: Jossey-Bass.

Hartley, J. and Betts, L. (2009) 'Publishing before the Thesis: 58 Postgraduate Views', *Higher Education Review*, 41(3), 29–44.

Kamler, B. and Thomson, P. (2006) *Helping Doctoral Students Write: Pedagogies for Supervision*, London: Routledge.

Kamler, B. and Thomson, P. (2008) 'The Failure of Dissertation Advice Books: Towards Alternative Pedagogies for Doctoral Writing', *Educational Researcher,* 37 (8), 507–18.

Kemmis, S. (2009) 'Understanding Professional Practice: A Synoptic Framework', in B. Green (ed.) *Understanding and Researching Professional Practice*, Rotterdam: Sense Publishers, pp. 19–39.

Lee, A. and Aitchison, C. (2009) 'Writing for the Doctorate and Beyond,' in D. Boud and A. Lee (eds) *Changing Practices of Doctoral Education*, London: Routledge, pp. 87–99.

Lee, A. and Green, B. (1997) 'Pedagogy and Disciplinarity in the "New" University', *UTS Review*, 3 (1), 1–25.

Lee, A. and Kamler, B. (2008) 'Bringing Pedagogy to Doctoral Publishing', *Teaching in Higher Education,* 13 (5), 511–23.

Lusted, D. (1986) 'Why Pedagogy?', *Screen*, 27 (5), 2–14.

McGrail, M., Rickard, C., and Jones, R. (2006) 'Publish or Perish: A Systematic Review of Interventions to Increase Academic Publication Rates', *Higher Education Research and Development,* 25 (1), 19–35.

Nerad, M. (2006) 'Globalization and its Impact on Research Education: Trends and Emerging Best Practices for the Doctorate of the Future', in M. Kiley and G. Mullins (eds) *Quality in Postgraduate Research: Knowledge Creation in Testing Times,* ANU: Canberra, pp. 5–12.

Park, C. (2007) *Redefining the Doctorate*, London: Higher Education Academy, www.hea.ac.uk

Peseta, T. (2007) 'Troubling our Desires for Research and Writing within the Academic Development Project', *International Journal for Academic Development,* 12 (1), 15–23.

QAA (2007) *Report on the Review of Research Degree Programmes: England and Northern Ireland*, http://www.qaa.ac.uk/search/publications/default.asp?order=1andsearch=review (accessed 23 June 2009).

Schatzki, T. R. (2001) 'Introduction: Practice Theory', in T. Schatzki, K. Knorr Cetina and E. von Savigny (eds) *The Practice Turn in Contemporary Theory*, London: Routledge, pp. 1–14.

Woodrow Wilson National Fellowship Foundation (2000) *Responsive PhD Project*, www.woodrow.org/responsivephd/ (accessed 12 June 2009).

Chapter 2

When the article is the dissertation

Pedagogies for a PhD by publication

Alison Lee

Introduction

Alison: Do you remember the conversation we had about how uncertain you were at that time about what your research was about?

Anna: Yeah, I remember.

Alison: I got a sense at that time that you were writing an article almost before you knew what you were doing, to some degree. Can you talk a bit about that?

Anna: Yeah, I think I presented my first articles and then I presented my . . . preliminary findings . . . and I remember when I was standing there it was like, 'oh no, I shouldn't have presented these findings' because they were so new to me and I was so unsure of what I was saying and how I should develop it. So I felt when I was doing the presentation, I remember that I felt really insecure about the new findings that I had for my second article. I also think it was a thing for me, you know, presenting my – I think the whole thing – presenting in English, the second time that I'm presenting my research in an international community and I knew who you guys were, the whole thing, but presenting results almost a bit too early, you know?

At the time I had this conversation with Anna, she was in the last semester of her PhD in a large Swedish university. The incident we are discussing occurred several years earlier, in the second year of her candidature, when she visited my university and presented a seminar. Anna is reflecting on what had been a difficult but decisive moment in her doctoral studies, when she became aware, through painful exposure, of what she did not yet know about her research. This moment served as a prompt for a series of critical conversations about the risks and benefits of 'going public' while undertaking a doctoral research degree.

Anna had chosen to undertake her doctorate as a 'PhD by publication'. The requirements for this course of study included four journal articles in international peer-reviewed journals, brought together into a compilation for examination with an exegesis, or 'cover story', that gives an account of the collection, the research that informed the production of the articles, and the 'doctoralness' of the body of work submitted in the portfolio for examination.[1]

So Anna's 'going public' was built into both the process and the outcome of the doctorate. She agreed to share her experience of undertaking doctoral study in this mode, including a series of discussions, in person and by Skype, in English, with me and one of her supervisors, Patrizia. Patrizia contributed her experiences and insights into the pedagogical practices involved in the development of Anna's doctorate, and Anna also made available details of the review process, including reviewers' reports and revision of the submitted articles. Reflecting here on her experience of this incident, and others along the way, Anna is able to assess the development of her understandings of her research and the relationships among the different elements of her doctoral portfolio. Her experience offers a fascinating insight into the risky yet productive experience of undertaking a PhD by publication, through which she is cast into the international arena of peer review from an early stage in her study.

Since these discussions were conducted, Anna has successfully completed and 'defended' her doctoral thesis, and has now graduated with a PhD. Patrizia and Anna continue to work together on projects within the department. In this chapter I re-present these dialogues around Anna's PhD as a way to explore a set of questions about the nature of doctoral writing, and the kinds of issues that arise when the conception of the final product of a social sciences PhD is not a single monograph or book-length dissertation but a series of shorter pieces, which are assessed by a range of different readers and reviewers before they are submitted for a final examination. These questions concern when and how the learnings and emerging understandings of a doctoral student, seen as a kind of 'trainee' as well as a bona fide researcher, should be made public; the consequences of decisions taken in relation to this question; and what pedagogical work supports the progression into full public appearance of the outcomes of the research undertaken.

My purpose in doing so is twofold. First, a close examination of one doctoral graduate's experience is a useful way to make visible and articulate some of the often conflicting positions taken within the field of doctoral education about what is and is not an appropriate outcome for a period of doctoral study. The PhD, as a kind of 'gold standard' for the highest award offered by the university, is replete with deeply held beliefs about what is necessary and sufficient as evidence of doctoral 'standard' (Lee, Brennan and Green, 2009). At the same time, however, it is changing and metamorphosing rapidly into a wide variety of different forms of output and different 'routes' to the attainment of a doctoral qualification (Park, 2007). Through such an exploration, it becomes possible to show how the space of doctoral pedagogy is a contested space, because the debates over what the doctorate is and what it is for, how it is evidenced and how this is changing, are themselves contested, unstable and changing rapidly. Many of these debates and struggles are over the artefacts produced by doctoral students for examination – the texts that evidence the successful production of knowledge. By extension, therefore, many of these struggles are experienced over writing, as a means whereby knowledge is encoded and 'staged' for reading, examination and wider dissemination.

Second, this account situates Anna's personal experiences of undertaking her PhD by publication within its institutional setting, in which an explicit curriculum infrastructure has been developed to support this kind of doctoral undertaking. This infrastructure scaffolds a set of more or less explicitly articulated pedagogical strategies within the supervisory relationship that address the particular nature of the writing constituting a doctorate of this kind. There are few close-up accounts of doctoral students undertaking this form of doctoral education in the literature that address the centrality of a public peer review process as a direct and central part of the doctoral curriculum. Anna's reflections on her experience, in dialogue with two senior researchers, Patrizia in Sweden and myself in Australia, represent an addition to the public record on these matters. All of these reflections, notably, involve close attention to the writing, review, revision and re-writing of the texts that are being produced simultaneously for examination and publication.

I have been teaching and researching in doctoral education for many years. One of the most persistent features of the experience of working in this area is the continuing anxiety about changes to what are seen as traditional and immutable forms and modes of engagement in scholarly work at this level. The attachment to the one-to-one relationship between a supervisor and a student, particularly in the humanities, is one of these sites of anxiety. Another is a curious reluctance to open the pedagogical space to empirical examination; and a third is the deeply held set of beliefs about the necessary value and benefit of engaging in the single extended dissertation as the primary outcome and evidence of the successful completion of a period of doctoral training. Even as the hyper-rationalities of quality assessment and measurement of capabilities and attributes have sought to break down older, more implicit, modes of exchange of doctoral artefacts and doctoral standards and values, the disciplinary and collegiate cultures of an older idea of the university persist in this sphere as in no other (Golde and Walker, 2006; Green, 2009; Lee and Green, 2009).

In the following sections, I locate and explore the conversations about Anna's experiences of writing and publishing her doctoral research by first introducing the PhD by publication in the context of the Swedish system of higher education. I then re-present some aspects of the particular pedagogical work discussed in these conversations, drawing on Anna's and Patrizia's accounts to articulate a conceptualization of a doctoral curriculum as 'rhetorical', not just in a narrower sense of learning particular academic and disciplinary discourses, but more fundamentally as involving relations of self and other, which shift and change through the course of the doctoral study.

The PhD by publication in Sweden

The PhD by publication is common in Scandinavian countries, one of a range of options for designing a doctoral output. Though it has more recently grown in scope in other countries such as the UK (Park, 2007), it remains marginal to the main mode of output, the single extended dissertation. The Swedish National Agency for Higher Education (2009) identifies two kinds of doctoral dissertations thus:

> There are two different kinds of dissertation: monographs and compilations. A monograph is a dissertation written as a unified and coherent work. Such dissertations are most common in non-laboratory subjects. Dissertations are almost exclusively monographs in the humanities, theology and law.
> Compilation dissertations comprise a number of papers written during the period of postgraduate training and a summary of the articles. Approximately two-thirds of all theses take this form.

The agency goes on to note that laboratory and clinical disciplines consist almost exclusively of compilations of articles, published or on their way to being published. Although a proportion of the articles in the dissertation may have been co-authored with other researchers, the majority of the submitted work has to be sole-authored by the PhD student, who must normally be the principal author of a major part of the dissertation. The summary, or 'cover story', is written independently, in a form that is accessible to non-specialists (Swedish National Agency for Higher Education, 2009).

In the space opened up by the concept of the 'compilation' or 'portfolio', new and flexible forms of knowledge products can be developed to represent graduates' achievement of research capabilities as well as tangible or concrete forms of their doctoral output (Clerke and Lee, 2008; Green, 2009). These in turn raise new questions about addressivity and publication and are part of more general debates about the purpose and outcome of a doctorate. More recently, in the international policy arena, these debates have shifted focus beyond the traditional textual product itself (the *dissertation*) to encompass the notion of doctoral capabilities (the production of the *researcher*). These are articulated in statements of doctoral 'descriptors' (e.g. the Dublin Descriptors in relation to the Bologna Process, 2006), and to outcomes descriptors in national qualification frameworks.

The Swedish National Agency for Higher Education has this to say about these debates:

Public debate about the scope of a dissertation has a long history, and has been full of vicissitudes. Should it represent a life's work or be part of a program of training and a first relatively comprehensive research assignment?

The latter view has come to dominate the discussion and the recent reform in postgraduate training emphasizes that what is involved is a program of education that should be completed within a relatively limited period of time. The PhD is a kind of journeyman's certificate, evidence that the postgraduate has the capacity to conduct research.

This notion of the 'journeyman' (sic) and the idea of doctoral candidature as a period of research 'training' raise important questions about the 'evidence' of a doctoral graduate's capacity to conduct research. In the case of the PhD by publication, what is foregrounded is the evidence of the doctoral graduate's capacity to articulate the outcomes of his or her research in public form, legitimized by the mechanisms of peer review. What has not often been made explicit is that it is rhetorical capacity – writerly capacity – that is a key component of what will count. The relationships among researching, writing and publishing are rarely teased out, nor are they commonly articulated or supported in a curriculum that is explicitly rhetorical. In Anna's doctoral story, there are some useful clues as to the nature of an explicitly rhetorical curriculum supporting writing for publication.

The conversations with Anna and Patrizia emphasize over and over the importance of a public debate within the department about each individual doctoral student's programme, and the importance of the curriculum infrastructure, principally the seminars, in supporting the model of publication. For example, in the department where Anna studied, there has to be agreement among the senior researchers about how many articles should make up the thesis. These researchers are not supervisors, or even members of a supervisory panel in the North American sense, but members of the research group in which the doctoral research is located, and with a stake in shaping the focus and monitoring and fostering the best possible quality of research. The standard number of articles is four, though that could be increased to five if necessary. Agreement is also required on how many need to be published or accepted before the student is deemed to be ready for the public defence and hence completion of the doctorate. The normal expectation is at least two papers either published or accepted and two manuscripts that could be submitted and under review. Additionally, agreement has to be reached on the criteria for the 'cover story'. At each stage, the curriculum is negotiated through the process of peer review and thus the PhD is clearly seen as a 'collective responsibility' (Chambaz, 2008). Further, the seminars are the place where the work in progress is shared and the negotiations carried out.

Conceptualizing the rhetorical curriculum

The conception of a 'rhetorical curriculum' that I use to examine Anna's stories of her doctoral experiences is an extension of Green's (1993) work on curriculum and literacy, in which he argues that 'language, "Writing" and the symbolic order are crucial considerations for understanding curriculum and schooling' (Green, 1993: 5). The educational concept of 'curriculum' is useful for understanding the complex knowledge work being undertaken within the doctorate (McWilliam and Singh, 2002; Lee, 2005; Gilbert, 2009). Gilbert (2009: 54) construes doctoral curriculum in terms of 'the forms of knowledge in which it is grounded, and how these are articulated in the documentation of the degree'. Further to this, Green and Cormack (in press) argue the centrality of language and writing to curriculum, understood in terms of 'textuality, representation, signification and symbolic practice, and more generally in terms of the social dynamics of discourse and subjectivity'.

The conception of curriculum that I am working with here is an over-arching term referring to all of the elements that make up the experience of undertaking a doctoral degree. Curriculum is concerned with knowledge, pedagogical relationships and the environment in which the research and learning take place. Doctoral curriculum includes planned activities such as seminars, workshops and groups, the individual and joint work of supervision, and an array of unplanned, informal or incidental events or activities that shape the experience of the doctoral student.

The conception of the 'rhetorical curriculum' is one that attends centrally to the work of discourse, representation and the dialogic:

> Life by its very nature is dialogic. To live means to participate in dialogue: to ask questions, to heed, to respond, to agree, and so forth. In this dialogue a person participates wholly and throughout his whole life: with his eyes, lips, hands, soul, spirit, with his whole body and deeds. He invests his entire self in discourse, and this discourse enters into the dialogic fabric of human life, into the world symposium.
>
> (Bakhtin, 1984: 293)

This conception draws attentions to one of the primary elements of doctoral research: that it is new knowledge that will live in the public arena through publication in scholarly forums. The distinction between doctoral knowledge work and that of undergraduate or masters degrees is that the work will be judged in terms of its contribution to the field of knowledge or practice that it inhabits. This involves centrally the assessment of the work by peers. In this sense, doctoral work must always attend to this requirement to be addressing a specialist community. One of the key terms in Bakhtin's theory of dialogism is 'addressivity' – the quality of directing an utterance to someone. This addressivity is at the heart of being rhetorical – communicating a meaning and an intention to someone.

The PhD by publication arguably has the concept of addressivity hard-wired into its structure and *raison d'être*. The article *is* the dissertation; the published work is addressed to an international scholarly readership as well as to a set of examiners and, along its way, to peers within the department, through seminars and conferences. It is arguably an extreme form of doctoral programme, with apparently fewer of the buffers between self and other, private and public, than are expected of a student undertaking doctoral training, or apprenticeship.

The Skype conversations among Anna, Patrizia and myself have occurred in the context of conducting an online doctoral education network and we continue to meet online, and through other technologies, to advance the work of the network. The process of reflecting on the interviews, and on the problematics it addresses, has itself been iterative and dialogic. It is also symptomatic, I suggest, of a troubling of the stability of the concepts of public and private in the circumstances of doing doctoral research in the globalized and technologized scholarly environment of the contemporary university. Curriculum, writing, addressivity, all shift and change in this context, and so too do the ideas of the 'self' that are being produced through the rhetorical practices of the curriculum.

In relation to Anna's PhD account of the production of her articles, I have been able to discern eight distinct, though inter-related, elements of the pedagogy enacted through supervision and through the broader curriculum infrastructure of formal and work-in-progress seminars discussed in the previous section:

1 designing the research with separable publishable elements;
2 analysing data with a view to writing up findings or understandings as publishable articles;
3 researching and selecting journals to target;
4 drafting the article with supervisors' assistance;
5 preparing drafts for presentation at work-in-progress seminars and de-briefing the presentations;
6 responding to the reviewers' comments with a view to resubmitting the article so that it succeeds in being accepted for publication;
7 resubmitting the article for publication; at the same time as
8 making explicit the rhetorical and conceptual learning that is accomplished through the experience of each article.

In the following two sections, I focus on the two key formal pedagogical underpinnings of these elements: the seminars and the supervision practices that focus on preparation of an article and response to reviewers' comments. These facilitate the processes of learning, data analysis, writing and publication, in which the movement from supervision to seminar is iterative and developmental. My aim is to demonstrate the overtly rhetorical nature of the pedagogical strategies and processes in this doctoral curriculum.

Seminars as rhetorical training grounds

The doctoral curriculum in Anna's department was tightly structured around a series of seminars. These were tied into the assessment and examination structures, interlocking with supervision relationships that were, as often as possible, closely connected to the actual research the supervisors were undertaking. The pedagogies enacted in supervision worked in tandem with the formal seminars and another set of seminars that were called work-in-progress seminars, which were attended by all of the available active researchers in the department, staff and doctoral students.

The formal seminars punctuate the different stages of the candidature. First, there is an initial series of courses that assists the preparation of the research proposal. The formal structure embedded in the department then requires three formal seminars. First comes a '30 per cent seminar', where the research proposal is discussed among the cohort of students and supervisors. This is followed by a '60 per cent seminar', which involves the participation of one of the committee members who will take part in the final committee for approving the thesis. That would normally be a representative from the department. This is seen as a crucial way for the department to participate in the development of the doctoral student's programme of research at the stages of the early plans, the early development and then the final product. At this seminar it is 'normal procedure' for the student to present all of the work completed to that point: the research plan, materials and work in progress, and plans for the next stages in the research. Finally, at the '90 per cent seminar' a discussant from outside the department is invited.

These formal seminars mark major structural elements in the 'spine' of this curriculum and are well attended by members of the department. In addition, there are regular, more informal, 'work-in-progress' seminars that are attended by members of the particular research group, academics and doctoral students. Patrizia describes how all of the researchers in their research group are included in the planning of this seminar programme each semester. An email is circulated to all group members, including the doctoral students, for anyone who has a paper in progress, who would like to be put on the list for a seminar, to put their name forward to present. Students become accustomed to work-in-progress seminars being 'normal business' – 'the way scholarly work is produced', as Patrizia put it. This is explicitly public and rhetorical pedagogy, the inculcation, in even beginning students, of the sense that, in the normal course of developing research, 'you have an idea, you sketch it down and you open it for comments from others to get some help to articulate it and also to critique it'.

Several elements distinguish this seminar-based curriculum, both the formal and the in-house work-in-progress events. The first is the organic connection between the doctoral students and the researchers. In Sweden, doctoral students are employed by the university for five years, to study and work full time, as employees. The kind of work undertaken might be teaching-, research- or administration-related work. This employment condition creates the possibility of collegial, rather than attenuated, structurally differentiated relationships. In addition, the doctoral students are organically involved in undertaking research in areas close to the major projects being undertaken by the academics who supervise them. Anna comments that she always saw herself as 'one of the staff members' and contrasts this with the experiences of many of the doctoral students she has met in her travels abroad.

The rhetorical nature of this curriculum is made explicit by the ways in which Patrizia talks about the purposes and the pedagogical work of the seminars:

> *Patrizia*: It is where the student is put in a situation where he or she has to formulate what the issue is, what the problem is and how she is thinking about this in the context of a doctoral thesis. To be presenting to others these thoughts and trying them out. This is how I try to think about this and also to then receive the comments on how the work is taken up by others.

This account exemplifies the addressivity at the very heart of this process: the student is required to present what she is thinking about her topic at the point at which she is attempting to formulate her problem and try out her thoughts. For this to work, there needs to be a clear and shared pedagogical purpose and way of operating.

The particular importance of the work-in-progress seminars is stressed over and over again by Patrizia: they lie 'at the very heart of our doctoral education within our specific field or our specific research interest'. Central to the success of these regular seminars as a curriculum space, in which important pedagogical work is done, is a culture of openness and trust among members and a sense of the research process as collective and dialogic:

> *Patrizia*: And that is so crucial in relation to pedagogy because if you are fostering a seminar culture that is all set about finding the flaws taking people's work down, then it's absolutely necessary to think in that way to protect your doctoral students not to showing their baby too soon because they will be killed. But if you think of it in a pedagogical way you would not see – you would not emphasize the bringing down side of the critique but rather trying to find a constructive way. Well someone

put in a flaw here, what can we do about this – how could we help this text become better? That is absolutely the culture that you need to grow. You cannot just say that this is not good, you have to present an argument, how can you help this text to become better.

What can be seen here is a glimpse of the responsibilities all group members need to have to do developmental, constructive work. To see the group process in the seminars as a site for pedagogy is to understand that these discursive practices are in themselves rhetorical. The seminar space is one where students learn to take risks in attempting to articulate emerging work. They also learn to address others: first, those to whom the text is directly addressed as fellow researchers and, second, those 'target' addressees in the public domain. These are the thesis 'opponents' before whom they will defend their thesis, the journal reviewers, editors and the international scholarly readership. The texts presented are in many respects emergent, incomplete, interim texts – texts on their way to somewhere else, text becoming fully rhetorical:

> *Patrizia*: The same manuscript could be presented several times as we would see an early draft where data analysis has started and the categories of the result is developing and the seminar group could help in that phase of the data analysis. And then it could also be presented later on as more a draft for a full manuscript containing all of the parts, bits and pieces that should be in a manuscript that you think of sending off for a journal article.

This notion of interim textuality is critical to understanding the pedagogical role of these seminars. The seminar space is a space of addressivity, a public space, but a provisional, developmental one, one that bridges and scaffolds the text and the writer from a private space of first exploration to more public and formal modes of articulation. The texts presented are always on their way to somewhere else, to addressing someone else.

Anna experiences the seminars as opportunities for her to practise the rhetorical work she needs to do in developing each of her articles along the course of her candidature. Before she develops and submits a manuscript of an article that has been prepared from part of her longitudinal study, she has presented it in various drafts over the entire length of its development. The group's feedback has scaffolded the development of the manuscript and offered practice in critique. Here she reflects on the difference between that experience and one of not having written work assessed by external audiences before submitting the final work for examination:

> *Anna:* I was complaining with one of my colleagues . . . I think I'd got some reviews back and they weren't . . . I think it was for the first article,

some of the reviewers . . . there were so many revisions for that article. But anyway, I told my colleagues about it and one of my colleagues said, Anna, this thing about writing a dissertation by publication, it's like you get walnuts all the time thrown at yourself, small walnuts, but if you write a monograph you get coconuts in the end. I don't know which one is best.

Anna contrasts this with her experience of engaging with the presentation of a student who is writing an extended dissertation without having published their work:

Anna: So when they talk about their text, their own text, it's hard to explain but they relate more to themselves. . . . I just know that when they're presenting, sometimes they don't get the comments they want to have because they can't show the whole picture, you know, they present one part of their monographs but sometimes they get – because it's harder to get comments on, because yeah. It's not there in the whole because they're a separate – they're taking out from the whole context of the whole monograph. You really need the whole monograph to give more good comments I guess.

When you write the articles, you have the aim and you have the theory and you have the method and you have the results and then you have the discussion. So hopefully they can see where it's going.

Supervisors and other members of the research group participate in the seminars and model the practices of listening and engaging in a developmental way. At times they are inviting students to open up areas for exploration; at other times they participate as 'opponents' at different points in the process. Anna articulates what she has learned from this process:

Anna: What I have really learned most – and it is really difficult – is to listen to a piece of presentation – on its own terms – and not in terms of what I think or what I think it should be, but in the terms that the person might be trying to think about. I learned that from being in the seminars and listening to what the others would say.

Patrizia encapsulates the collective responsibility of the whole research group in this developmental process:

Patrizia: Of course, along the way, when the articles are being produced, there are also some others involved in looking at the depth and quality and richness in this and those are the reviewers from the international research community and these various things, I think, contribute to a lot more transparency throughout the research work, that you get involved. It's not only a process between the supervisor and the student, but there's actually a whole international research community involved looking after the quality in what is being published.

The idea of the 'rhetorical curriculum' here draws attention to the carefully scaffolded staging of the movement from collective preliminary development work to the more private space of the student-writer–supervisor-reader relationship and back out to staged semi-public and increasingly public presentations of the developing work. Thus there is always, explicitly, another, or others, to whom the writing is addressed.

Rhetorical supervision pedagogies

The supervision of Anna's PhD was undertaken by two senior researchers, Patrizia and Erik, who had been working on a large research project over the previous eight years. Anna's research was a continuation of that larger research work and consisted of a longitudinal study in the area of professional identity formation. Each of the four articles she wrote was reporting on one phase of the longitudinal study, although the last two articles located the specific focus of the whole study more generally. The 'cover story' reflected on how conceptual, methodological and substantive developments and changes occurred over the lifetime of the research and Anna's candidature.

I asked how the shaping of the doctorate in terms of journal articles influenced the way the research was developed. The response was in terms of seeing the research as a *design issue*. Several key principles emerged from the discussion. First, the overall research topic had to lend itself to separate components being developed along the way. Attention had to be given to milestones or elements that could be separately presented as articles. In Anna's case, four inter-related studies were designed that addressed a particular research question.

Anna comments on the particular discipline of having to work within the rhetorical and scale constraints of a journal article at the same time as she is grappling with her data analysis:

> *Anna:* I mean writing in article format you have a certain amount of words and you have to be short and concise and I remember the first article I wrote, I think I had written 11 pages and I remember for this, I was going to meet Patrizia and Erik and I remember Erik said to me, 'Anna, this ten lines you have here' – and he pointed like at page five or something like that – 'this is what your article could be about' because the other things – because you have to be quite short and you can't be all over the place.

Anna was able to see that the 10 pages she had been writing had functioned to help her to make sense of the data and to clarify her own ideas about what the article's focus might become. Erik's advice was rhetorical, in the sense that he directed her attention to what might be relevant in relation to the journal article.

In the context of the Skype conversations with Patrizia and me, Anna is able to articulate her writing process:

> *Anna*: I think that's how I normally start out. I mean I write a little bit all over the place and then I talk to them and they help me see what I have written and then I start rewriting it and then I rewrite this and we have a meeting again. I don't know how many times we meet, maybe two times a month maybe.
>
> But I always – for me, talking about my research and talking about my writing and how I should write has been, it's when I feel like I develop. Because when I talk about it I can see what I mean or they can point to certain issues, here you have to develop or you should take this away or what do you mean here. Then it becomes clear to me what I'm actually doing.

The point at which an article is ready to send off to a journal for review is a matter for negotiation. Patrizia notes that the supervisors work, together with the student, with a manuscript to the point at which what is needed is an outside eye: 'it's time for sending it off and getting comments from reviewers who can see things that I cannot see'. Patrizia uses an English translation of a Swedish expression for the risks of only the writer and her supervisors seeing the re-written article: 'you risk getting – home blind – you don't see flaws within your own home because you're so used to seeing them'. Interestingly, whereas there is clearly a risk for the student in having her work peer reviewed in an international context alongside the work of more experienced writers, Patrizia sees a parallel risk of the doctoral student remaining parochial in terms of the addressivity of the work.

A key element in the pedagogical process of working with the articles involves the moment when the review comments from the international research community are received. Patrizia reports that she and Erik adopted the following set of procedures with Anna, as with other doctoral students, based on their experience that most, if not all, articles submitted by doctoral students require some revision following review. First, Anna is told to read and think about the comments from the reviewers and then set a date for a supervision meeting. Patrizia and Erik listen to what Anna thinks is the main critique that the reviewers have made, what she thinks about that, why the critique has been made and what she believes could be done to revise the article. Patrizia notes:

Patrizia: It's really important I think that the students have the first go in looking at that and there is something psychological in that not to be intimidated by the list of comments but try to look at it with a sort of clear sighted view and take it seriously and think about what kind of critique is there.

Then, in supervision, the three will compare notes and come to an agreement about what needs to be done. There is a training involved, on how to read and act on reviewers' comments; a kind of literacy is required that can interpret the critique in an appropriate perspective. Patrizia described pedagogical strategies for developing this kind of literacy:

Patrizia: Sometimes the doctoral students don't see what is really a serious critique and what could more easily be taken on. So we will have a discussion on why it's a serious critique or if it's not. Then we will advise the doctoral student to make a sort of a table to try and list all the comments from the reviewers on the one side and list on the other side all the amendments that will be done.

In those cases where the students or where we together think that this is not really an issue then we will ask Anna to write an argument as to why we will not change that because it would fit within the bigger plan or the reviewer might have misunderstood or something like that. So we see to it that every comment is taken care of. That is how we would work with reviews coming in.

Several important questions arise regarding the differences in this process from the process of a more experienced writer responding to reviewers and revising an article. In the case of the experienced writer, there is only one task to do, which is to revise the article so that it can be successfully resubmitted and accepted for publication. The pedagogical work of helping a doctoral student, in contrast, is both to successfully revise the article and also to develop the skills and experiences of writing, often in English, for an international readership in the interim phases of completing a doctoral research project.

How do supervisors bring the work of developing the skills of the doctoral student together with the practical task of addressing the reviewer's comments? When a doctoral student is going through a process of learning about becoming a researcher, what kind of strategies need to be adopted? How is the developmental process as well as the textual revision process managed? What does that pedagogy look like? Part of the issue here is that each article is part of a larger research project, as well as being part of a training process:

Patrizia: Well of course you have to keep an eye on the whole – I mean the plot, the synopsis that has been set out for the whole research program or the doctoral thesis if you like – so that you cannot just address each comment as if it was the singular comment. It has to fit in with the whole conceptualization of the doctoral thesis and it is really important that the student also understands that and thinks about the comments in relation to that.

Anna is clear about this need to be attending to part–whole relations in her writing at all points in the development of articles:

Anna: But at the same time, it feels like everything fits quite well together and it feels like I don't – I don't think my articles are spread over a huge field, you know? I think they're similar in a way and I can see a thread. But I have to say, sometimes in the whole process I actually saw the articles, you know?

In 'seeing' the articles, Anna sees the development of a sequence of pieces that fit together, at the same time as being distinct because they are each published separately, addressing different readerships and participating in different debates in her field.

Debating the PhD by publication

In countries outside Scandinavia, the idea of a PhD by publication is sometimes seen to be problematic – counter-intuitive, even. The traditional idea of the single extended dissertation is one to which scholars – in human science disciplines at least – are deeply attached. This account of Anna's doctoral experience can help to tease out a little why this kind of doctoral structure might represent some kind of challenge or disruption to the scheme of things or how things are meant to be in the rarefied atmosphere of the doctorate, that 'pinnacle of educational attainment' (Gilbert, 2009: 54) of the modern university.

What are opponents of publication-based doctorates worried about? Some of the questions that arise when alternatives to the traditional extended single dissertation are put forward evince concern or even fear that something is being lost in the rush to diversification and the public sphere. Will there be enough in-depth analysis, given that the writing is broken into discrete pieces and not argued through? Is there something intrinsic to the extended dissertation writing process that *in itself* produces a necessary deep engagement with a topic and an argument? Can this deep engagement be achieved in short pieces of writing? How would we know? These are the kinds of objections voiced by respondents in a survey undertaken in 1998 by the UK Council for Graduate Education (1998).[2] Though much has changed in terms of the advent of diverse routes to the doctorate in the UK (see Park, 2007), there is no more recent survey that canvasses changes in view since the time of this first survey.

Other anxieties are more explicitly pedagogical and concern the staging of the learning and understanding of the novice researcher. Are students given enough time to learn what they need to know if they are being required to move to a public arena early in their doctoral research? What are the risks? What curricular and pedagogical scaffolding needs to be in place to support the production of publishable outputs along the way towards completing the research? These questions are taken up by Paré in the next chapter.

I put these questions to Anna and Patrizia in our interview, in an attempt to generate an explicit rebuttal. What was interesting is that the issues I raised made little sense to either of them. For them, the design of the study and the strong and explicit framework in which Anna worked offered a robust way to build the research; moreover, the undertaking of the research and its publication in an international arena were an almost seamless progression. Anna's experience is of course only one case, but the way it played out for her appeared to be an articulation of her experience of how business was done in this environment.

What pedagogical work surrounds and supports a successful PhD by publication? Often, what I see in my experience as a researcher and teacher in doctoral education is that students who want to publish their research, and to complete their doctorate through a plan of publications, are left without the necessary pedagogical and environmental infrastructure. That is, their experience is of an unskilled, ad hoc, unplanned and information-poor environment. Becoming rhetorical – that is, learning how to position one's work within a community of scholars, to address a readership of peers – is largely left to chance. Kamler's chapter on publication brokering (Chapter 5 of this volume) is one strategy for addressing this problem.

What is different for Anna is the explicitly rhetorical curriculum: the clear imperative to share work with others, the detailed structure with regular, staged opportunities and requirements to present work and to give and receive feedback, the strong and deliberate scaffolding, the integration of Anna and her doctoral peers into the culture of the research group and the department, the explicit publication-focused pedagogy of supervision, and a relationship of respect and trust in the process of articulating developing thoughts.

Anna is very clear that these things are not always present in the experiences of her peers in other places, and about what makes the difference for her. She speaks of 'daring to present your work and feel comfortable and safe in the group'. And she speaks clearly about the distributed responsibility among all participants for making the seminar work. For her this is clearly a matter of the generous and generative exercise of power within the community of researchers who support the doctoral programme. Without these elements, Anna is clear that the publication of her work would have been much more difficult and less rewarding. Anna's positioning of herself as a successful published author in this narrative echoes the findings of a recent study by Hartley and Betts (2009) in which students who had published during their traditional (UK) doctoral candidature were also convinced of the value of doing so, despite some evidence that the work of writing for publication prolonged their candidature a little. With the curriculum work she has had to support her, Anna has experienced the high energy of her work being 'launched' into the public domain. As she says:

> *Anna*: I just have to say, the satisfaction that I've felt when I actually get something published is amazing. I've never been so proud of myself my whole life. I mean it's really – Patrizia saw me dancing in the corridor. It's a really big thing.

Notes

1 This degree needs to be to be clearly distinguished from a degree with a similar name, that is a degree awarded in recognition of a body of already published works (Park, 2007)
2 Sixty-three responses were received on behalf of faculties in 21 European countries (UKCGE, 1998: 11).

References

Bakhtin, M. (1984) *Problems of Dostoevsky's Poetic* (ed. and transl. C. Emerson), Minneapolis: University of Minnesota Press.

Bologna (2006) *Bologna Handbook*, Berlin: RAABE Academic Publishers.

Chambaz, J. (2008) 'Reforming Doctorate Education in Europe – a Response to Global Challenges', in M. Kiley and G. Mullins (eds) *Research Education in the New Global Environment*, Proceedings of the Quality in Postgraduate Research Conference, 17–18 April, Adelaide, Canberra: Centre for Educational Development and Academic Methods, The Australian National University, vol. 2, pp. 14–21.

Clerke, T. and Lee, A (2008) 'Mainstreaming the Doctoral Research Portfolio?', in M. Kiley and G. Mullins (eds) *Research Education in the New Global Environment*, Proceedings of the Quality in Postgraduate Research Conference, 17–18 April, Adelaide, Canberra: Centre for Educational Development and Academic Methods, The Australian National University, vol. 2, pp. 17–30.

Gilbert, R. (2009) 'The Doctorate as Curriculum: A Perspective on Goals and Outcomes of Doctoral Education', in D. Boud and A. Lee (eds) *Changing Practices of Doctoral Education*, London: Routledge, pp. 54–68.

Golde, C. M., and Walker, G. E. (2006) *Envisioning the Future of Doctoral Education: Preparing Stewards of the Discipline – Carnegie essays on the doctorate*, San Francisco, CA: Jossey-Bass.

Green, B. (ed.) (1993) *The Insistence of the Letter: Literacy Studies and Curriculum Theorizing*, London: Falmer Press.

Green, B. (2009) 'Changing Perspectives, Changing Practices: Doctoral Education in

Transition', in D. Boud and A. Lee (eds) *Changing Practices of Doctoral Education*, London, Routledge, pp. 239–48.

Green, B. and Cormack, P. (in press) 'Re-reading the Historical Record: Curriculum History and the Linguistic Turn', in B. Baker (ed.) *New Curriculum Histories*, Rotterdam: Sense Publishers.

Hartley, J. and Betts, L. (2009) 'Publishing before the Thesis: 58 Postgraduate Views', *Higher Education Review*, 41 (3), 29–44.

Lee, A. (2005) 'Thinking Curriculum: Framing Research/Education', in T. W. Maxwell, C. Hickey and T. Evans (eds) *Professional Doctorates: Working towards Impact*, Proceedings of the 5th Biennial International Conference on Professional Doctorates, Deakin University, Geelong.

Lee, A. Brennan, M. and Green, B. (2009) 'Re-imagining Doctoral Education: Professional Doctorates and Beyond', *Higher Education Research and Development*, 28 (3), 275–87.

Lee, A. and Green, B. (2009) 'Supervision as Metaphor', *Studies in Higher Education*, 34 (6), 615–30.

McWilliam, E. and Singh, P. (2002) 'Towards a Research Training Curriculum: What? Why? How? Who?', *Australian Educational Researcher*, 29 (3), 3–19.

Park, C. (2007) *Redefining the Doctorate*, London: Higher Education Academy, www.hea.ac.uk

Swedish National Agency for Higher Education (2009) 'PhD Studies: Research Training in Sweden', http://www.doktorandhandboken.nu/english (accessed 12 June 2009).

UK Council for Graduate Education (1998) *The Status of Published Work in Submissions for Doctoral Degrees in European Universities*, London: UKCGE.

Chapter 3

Slow the presses

Concerns about premature publication

Anthony Paré

> I am gripped with the anxiety of perhaps publishing too prematurely and therefore establishing a less-than-reputable name in my field(s).
>
> (Doctoral student journal entry)

As the chapters in this book indicate, the push to help doctoral students publish is motivated by a number of different forces, including the strongly pragmatic need to help students advance their careers in a period of intense competition for jobs, both within and outside the university. Scholarship juries, funding agencies and hiring committees all search for ways to divide applicants into the more or less desirable, and a list of publications identifies a promising newcomer. Although the imperative is undeniable, and the desire to help students is laudable, the dangers of rushing students into the public exposure of publication need to be considered.

Of course, the process of reaching publication can be deeply pedagogic as well as practical, but my experience as a doctoral supervisor, journal editor and teacher has shown me that the anxiety to publish can hamper rather than help students. Not so long ago, publication before graduation was rare. But as a journal editor I now receive an increasing number of submissions from graduate students intent on publishing their 200-page dissertations as 15-page articles. It is rarely difficult to identify the authors as doctoral students. The topics are far too broad for short papers, the research methodologies are extensive and longitudinal, the theoretical terminology is impenetrable, the parentheses are crammed with citations, and the reference list is half as long as the paper itself. In other words, the submissions are reasonable facsimiles of student or school genres, but ineffective journal articles. They display knowledge – the chief rhetorical goal of school discourse – but fail to address an actual dialogue among working scholars. And, as a teacher and supervisor, I sense an increase in publication-related anxiety among graduate students. In this chapter, I consider these and other dangers that might follow from pressure to publish, and I propose aspects of a doctoral pedagogy that might help remove or diminish their debilitating effects.

In the first section of the chapter, I consider how writing functions heuristically as a method of promoting thought – a key recognition of the early writing process movement described in Chapter 1. The argument here is fairly straightforward: writing isn't merely a means of expression, it's also a means of exploration and discovery. Student writing, in particular, should be inventive, speculative, provisional; students should be encouraged to take chances, to experiment, to improvise. The assumption is that such efforts to articulate complex and innovative ideas are powerful opportunities to learn. The pressure to publish might force student writers past this heuristic phase to a more public, more rhetorical stance, in which they are open to criticism, censure and rejection. Like the ESL student who avoids error by writing in simple sentences in the present tense, the doctoral student pushed to publish might avoid taking chances with form, topic and purpose.

In the second section of the chapter, I trace a further development in contemporary writing studies – the view of writing as situated social action – and consider how that understanding of writing also complicates the transition from student writer to publishing writer. The argument here takes a cultural and rhetorical turn: briefly, it proposes that valuable contributions to academic debates are the result of a deep immersion in a community's discourse – an immersion that happens over time through authentic engagement in an ongoing dialogue, and that happens *only* when a writer locates herself in the historical, ideological and intellectual threads of that dialogue. Rhetorical success requires an insider's knowledge of a discipline's genres, its arguments, its distinctive styles, its key thinkers and theories. To return to the ESL example: student writers often do not sound like native speakers of the disciplinary discourse. They over-stress the banal, under-stress the critical, misuse key terms and are soon revealed as newcomers.

Both the encouragement to use writing as an exploratory activity *and* insight into a discipline's rhetorical practice are likely to come from the student's doctoral supervisor, who directs the programme of study and, as Green notes, 'represents, or stands in for, the Discipline itself, and also the Academy' (2005: 162). In the chapter's third section, then, I draw on my own research into supervision and the dissertation to consider whether and how supervisors can facilitate the move to publication. A pedagogy devoted to hastening the transition from newcomer to publishing writer requires teachers who are capable of providing the explicit attention to and instruction in the rhetorical practices that such a pedagogy demands.

In the fourth and final section of the chapter, I describe aspects of a doctoral programme at my own institution that attempt to help students join their disciplinary conversations *before* graduation: first, by extensive experience of the heuristic power of writing (and speaking); second, by a close, even anthropological, attention to their communities' discourse; and, third, by a deep immersion in authentic rhetorical exchange, by which I mean participation in their disciplines' actual conversations. Neither genuine rhetorical contributions nor explicit attention to rhetorical practices are common experiences for doctoral students, as the literature indicates (e.g. Aitchison and Lee, 2006; Rose and McClafferty, 2001; Kamler and Thomson, 2006; Parry, 1998; Paré, Starke-Meyerring, and McAlpine, in press). But in this chapter I will argue that students who do engage in such participation and analysis are more likely to become both better readers and better writers: attentive to the arguments they hear, careful in those they craft and ready to join their disciplinary conversations.

Writing as heuristic

Writers don't simply express thoughts already formed in the mind; they *make* meaning as they compose. In Britton's (1980) memorable phrase, the writer is 'shaping at the point of utterance'. This view of writing promotes it from a mere scribal act to an epistemic activity that can be used to promote different ways or types of thinking and learning. Janet Emig, an early and influential proponent of writing-to-learn, argued that '[w]riting represents a unique mode of learning – not merely valuable, not merely special, but unique' (1977: 122). Although Emig recognized the heuristic power of language generally, she made a singular case for writing. And, although her distinctions between talk and writing were stated more strongly than they might be today, particularly with the mode-blurring effects of digital communications, her list of reasons for writing's special effects are difficult to refute, including: writing is slower and more deliberate ('self-rhythmed'); writing must create its own context; writers must conjure readers and anticipate responses; writing is visible and permanent and thus permits, even requires, reflection; and writing 'establishes explicit and systematic conceptual groupings through lexical, syntactic, and rhetorical devices' (ibid.: 128).

In other words, because the writer must foresee the situation into which her text will emerge (i.e. the goals, attitudes and expectations of her reader(s), the setting and the occasion of the reading etc.), and because written language and the craft of writing promote greater attention to conceptual sequence and cohesion than speech, the writer is forced to wrestle more carefully and deliberately with ideas. John Gage explained that dynamic relationship this way:

> Writing is thinking made tangible, thinking that can be examined because it is on the page and not in the head, invisible, floating around. Writing is thinking that can be stopped and tinkered with. It is a way of holding thought still long enough to examine its structures, its possibilities, its flaws. The road to a clearer understanding is travelled on paper. It is through an attempt to find words for ourselves in which to express related ideas that we often discover what we think.
>
> (1986: 24)

This description of writing was much elaborated in the work of those who espoused a 'cognitive process theory' of writing (e.g. Flower and Hayes, 1980, 1981). That theory, and the research it spawned, offered compelling evidence that expert writers use various forms of writing – brainstorming, outlining, freewriting – to play with ideas even before drafting, and that those strategies appear to help them reflect on their readers, goals and plans and to come to new understandings of their topics. Moreover, the research demonstrated that able writers remain open to new ideas, new plans and new formulations as they draft, and postpone final commitment to a public text far longer than less able writers, who get stuck in text production and editorial detail for what they appear to hope will be a first/final draft.

In our Writing Centre, in recognition of this heuristic power of writing, we give students licence to write a 'glorious failure', our name for the ambitious paper that doesn't quite reach its potential, but provides students with a challenging intellectual and rhetorical experience. We feel that the banal essays that students so often produce are the result of a caution born of years of guessing what teachers want and then receiving feedback in direct relation to the accuracy of their guess. Such texts, called 'textoids' by Russ Hunt (e.g. 1993), lack rhetorical or pragmatic force. Though ostensibly arguments, their actual purpose is revealed through their central role in education's ranking and sorting process: they are displays of knowledge, not contributions to a dialogue. Having become expert at error-avoidance, students take the safe path and write tepid, uncontroversial, bland papers designed to meet standards they are unable to express but have become proficient at achieving. Such school writing is arhetorical – it lacks real readers and serves little or no purpose beyond evaluation – and students are careful not to take chances, preferring instead to repeat what teachers might want to hear. We elicit 'glorious failures' not by asking for them but, rather, by encouraging students to write on topics about which they are expert, or wish to become expert, by giving them plenty of opportunities to talk and write about their topics in advance of drafting, by circulating finished papers to the entire class, and by receiving the texts as interested readers rather than judges. We see the reading, talking, thinking and writing that students engage in as the purpose and value of the task, and the textual product as only a secondary by-product of the students' learning. And, of course, some of the papers are not failures at all, but strong, effective statements that surprise and gratify us.

My point is that the rush to publication makes chance-taking less likely, and thus reduces the potential for a challenging and transformative rhetorical experience. The young author aiming for an editor's approval might take the cautious route, repeat or paraphrase already acceptable arguments, and avoid the conceptualizing that stretches the mind and produces valuable contributions. Publication encourages closure, or it can, and often turns writing from an exploration into a performance.

Entering the conversation

But writing is of course more than a tool for the personal exploration or elaboration of ideas; it is also the chief collective means of making knowledge in many areas of human activity. When we learn how to write within our academic disciplines, institutions or 'discourse communities' (Bizzell, 1992; Porter, 1992; Swales, 1990), we are learning to participate in a rhetorical practice with a history, implicit and explicit rules, specialized forums and formats, and contested terrain. Perhaps the passage that best captures this collective enterprise is Kenneth Burke's evocative description of the human conversation:

> Imagine that you enter a parlor. You come late. When you arrive, others have long preceded you, and they are engaged in a heated discussion, a discussion too heated for them to pause and tell you exactly what it is about. In fact, the discussion had already begun long before any of them got there, so that no one present is qualified to retrace for you all the steps that had gone before. You listen for a while, until you decide that you have caught the tenor of the argument; then you put in your oar. Someone answers; you answer him; another comes to your defense; another aligns himself against you . . . However, the discussion is interminable. The hour grows late, you must depart. And you do depart, with the discussion still vigorously in progress.
>
> (Burke, 1941: 110–11)

Each discourse community has its own ongoing conversation, each has a different tenor to its argument, and each produces its own particular perspective on the world. As Berlin put it, 'Knowledge . . . is a matter of mutual agreement appearing as the product of the rhetorical activity, the discussion, of a given discourse community' (1987: 166).[1] A central task of doctoral education, then, is to help students join the ongoing conversations of their disciplinary communities, a process that takes the kind of time and attention that Burke conjures here. Those conversations are historical: current debates cannot be well understood without an appreciation of their chronological and conceptual development – the defining moments, the schisms, the fallow periods, the years of rapid theoretical growth. Nor can they be fully grasped without a sense of the contemporary landscape: the various schools of thought, the conflicts and controversies, the key theories and their proponents, the relevant research.

If we think of our own intellectual development, especially in our fields of specialization, we may see this process as one of gradually finding a location in the conversation, or situating ourselves vis-à-vis others in the discussion. We may remember, for example, embracing a particular theory or theorist, only to discover that such an allegiance placed us in a school of thought opposed to another theory or theorist we admired. The deep immersion in a wide range of confirming and conflicting ideas is (or can be) typical of graduate studies, one that promotes complexity of thought and sensitivity to multiple perspectives. This, in turn, can lead to arguments that are more sophisticated, nuanced and alert to a variety of opinion and possibility.

Further complicating this picture of discursive variation across settings has been rhetorical genre theory, which was first articulated in Miller's 1984 article, 'Genre as Social Action' (see also Freedman and Medway, 1994; Berkenkotter and Huckin, 1995; Coe, Lingard and Teslenko, 2002).[2] This perspective views discipline-specific texts (such as academic articles or grant applications) as situated social actions – that is, as rhetorical strategies developed within discourse communities to produce relatively stable, regulated outcomes or consequences. The repetition or typification implied by the word 'genre' is thus extended beyond textual regularity to include patterns of iteration in the activities within which repeated texts operate. The physical text lies at the heart of the genre, but is only part of a larger, repeating practice. In effect, a genre is an attempt to regularize or reproduce a particular rhetorical situation, which, according to Bitzer (1968), includes the audience for the discourse, the exigence or motivating force that elicits the discourse, and the context or constraining conditions within which the utterance is made (including institutional or disciplinary regulations).

It is important to note that the influence of genre, in this new rhetorical account, stretches backward to the writer's composing process and forward to the reader's response to the text. As Bazerman puts it, 'A genre provides a writer with a way of formulating responses in certain circumstances and a reader a way of recognizing the kind of message being transmitted. A genre is a social construct that regularizes communication, interaction, and relations' (1988: 62). That is, invention, arrangement and style are discipline and situation specific, as are readers' responses to texts.

The ability to participate successfully in a genre as a writer and reader develops over time and through engagement. A critical lesson learned in this process, and a central feature of a rhetorical definition of genre, is *kairos*, the Greek word drawn from classical rhetoric that refers to timeliness in speech – that is, an understanding of both the opportune moment for speech and the appropriate utterance for the given circumstance: a sense of *when* to speak and *what* to say *at that moment*. A kairotic sensibility requires a rich and complex appreciation of rhetorical situations.

Supervision and apprenticeship

There has been debate in recent years about whether genres can be explicitly taught outside the sphere of their activity – that is, outside the rhetorical situations that they both create and address – or whether they can only be learned through situated participation (e.g. Freedman, 1993; Cope and

Kalantzis, 1993). Can workplace genres be taught in classrooms, or university genres taught in secondary school? Some research suggests that the rules governing participation in genres are learned gradually and tacitly in the process of becoming a member of a discourse community (e.g. McCarthy, 1987; Berkenkotter, Huckin and Ackerman, 1988; Freedman, 1987; MacKinnon, 1993; Prior, 1998; Dias, Freedman, Medway and Paré, 1999; Paré, 2002). However, doctoral students who aspire to the scholarly life *are already in* a version of their eventual workplace, and their education is the ultimate preparation for participation in that workplace. And those who end up working outside the university are, nonetheless, engaged in some of the ways of thinking and writing that are likely to animate the intellectual and rhetorical work of their eventual work settings. In other words, doctoral students are in a form of apprenticeship, working under the mentorship of (presumably) successful old-timers.

However, a doctoral pedagogy devoted to helping students move from apprenticeship to professional participation requires teachers with a deep understanding of the rhetorical practices of their disciplines. The problem this raises is described by Bazerman (in press):

> I have found smart, accomplished colleagues in other disciplines who have little vocabulary for discussing writing beyond the corrective grammar they learned in high school. Although [they] have learned the genres of their profession and are successful in them, their reflective ability to manipulate them is limited because of a lack of linguistic and rhetorical vocabulary.

A pedagogy that supports the publication of doctoral work requires pedagogues who are engaged in that activity – that is, teachers who 'have learned the genres of their profession and are successful in them' – *and* who are also able to induct students into their discipline's discourse practices. As part of an ongoing study of dissertation writing, I have recorded conversations between students and their supervisors and I have interviewed them, together and separately. Although some supervisors are remarkably articulate, others are not; consider this comment made by a supervisor to her student about the draft of a dissertation chapter:

> *Supervisor*: I've read what you've done and [can] tell you . . . my thoughts on how it might be somewhat strengthened, because I think the information is there but I have two main points about it. One is that it should be maybe a bit more focused. More focused on it being a chapter within a PhD thesis . . . The other general comment is to, I don't know, firm it up, I suppose. Because it's a data collection chapter, I'd like more numbers, I suppose . . . Kind of more strongly represent what you've done. So

my general feeling is that the chapter itself . . . should be put within a slightly bigger box for the committee.

Like the people that Bazerman mentions above, this is a 'smart, accomplished' colleague, one with many publications, and yet she struggles here to describe the rhetorical moves at which she herself is so adept. She seems unable to overcome the automaticity that is a hallmark of expertise; she can do it, but she can't explain it. Perhaps this is not surprising, since we know that fluency in language does not require expressible knowledge of the linguistic system employed, and the same seems likely for rhetorical skill: one can make an effective argument without being able to explain how one is doing it. But can a pedagogy for publishing be developed without instructors who have the ability to articulate the rhetorical practices that students are being asked to master? In the interview excerpt below, a supervisor admits that he holds students to standards that are of unknown origin:

Supervisor: It's a very formal exercise, undertaking research for a PhD, in presenting the work in the actual thesis, and so I need to sort of enforce certain conventions.

Interviewer: Right, and whose conventions are those? Where do those conventions come from?

Supervisor: Well I – that's an interesting question. I suppose they come to [student] filtered through me, so as a supervisor I suppose at the end of the day it's my view of what is a convention, and I suppose my view is formed partly by seeing other theses. But I'm not sure that's the answer. I'm not really sure where . . . I'm not sure I can answer it. I have a view. Obviously it must come from somewhere. But I don't know where. I don't know where we decide how we do this.

Research cited above (McCarthy, 1987; Berkenkotter, Huckin and Ackerman, 1988; Freedman, 1987; MacKinnon, 1993; Prior, 1998; Dias, Freedman, Medway and Paré, 1999; Paré, 2002) suggests that writers learn what they need to know by a gradual process of enculturation, a form of osmosis that occurs over time as newcomers become situated in a community's rhetorical action. This certainly seems true of writing in the academy, as each new generation of scholars first enters and then dominates the disciplinary conversation. But a pedagogy devoted to helping doctoral students publish *during* their programme of study assumes that the process of learning to participate in a discipline's discourse can be accelerated. How might that be accomplished? The following comments, made during a focus group discussion among doctoral students, begins to suggest an answer to that question:

[My committee] have pushed me to write and publish in ways that I wasn't necessarily ready, or considered myself able, to do. And they have worked me. They brought me on as an assistant editor on journals and on books, and that has allowed me to sort of really engage in the process by looking at the referee process and looking at my own writing and say, 'Oh, I can do this.' You know what I mean? And like, 'Yeah, you can do this and we want you to write in the next book or we want you to submit to this journal,' and being assertive in that regard. 'You are going to submit this year to a journal.' And so that is what happened. Eventually it happened. Here I am, you know, I'm finishing my program, I have nearly 10 publications, I've presented at almost a dozen conferences. These are things that I probably wouldn't have done on my own. I probably wouldn't have taken it upon myself. I probably would be getting at the stage right now of going to conferences or maybe I'd have been to a few or maybe I'd have one thing published, you know.

(Focus group discussion)

This student's level of engagement – as an assistant editor and new author – was promoted and supported by his doctoral committee members, whose own involvement in writing, editing and publishing allowed them to provide the student with a true, hands-on apprenticeship.

A pedagogy for writers

To sum up my argument: the value of exploratory writing and speaking as a means to greater understanding, the highly situated nature of successful contributions to disciplinary conversations, and the difficulty doctoral supervisors may have explaining the nature and dynamics of those conversations should make us cautious about pushing students to publication too quickly. But we cannot ignore the market pressure on students who must compete for jobs and scholarships, or the potential educational benefit of entering the debate in one's field. The question, then, is how to do that without short-circuiting or abbreviating the potentially enriching experience of writing-to-learn and the rhetorical chance-taking that leads to innovation and discovery.

In what follows, I describe aspects of a doctoral programme in my own institution, as well as a range of what might be called extra-curricular but complementary activities that seek to exploit the heuristic power of writing, locate writing at the centre of scholarly work, and offer students chances to engage in authentic academic discourse. The students in the programme represent a range of interests within the broad field of education, and a cohort might include students studying curriculum and youth culture, second-language education, literacy, classroom technologies, international education, non-formal teaching and learning, educational administration and other topics. The programme is highly individual – leaving the selection of a few elective courses up to the students, their supervisors and their committees – but there are three required courses: a research methodology course (selected from a list of different approaches to research) and two year-long PhD seminars, one in the first year of study and the other in the second year. One highly recommended elective course focuses on academic writing. Students are also required to write (and orally defend) two comprehensive questions framed in negotiation with their supervisor and committee and to defend the completed dissertation in a public *viva voce*. In addition, the dissertation is sent for external review to a well-known scholar in the student's field of study.

The two seminars are taken by students as a cohort, and their central purpose is to make explicit the transition from graduate student to scholar. Writing and the process of becoming an academic writer are main preoccupations of the seminars, which meet every other week from September to April, with a month-long break in December. A regular practice during the seminars is 'inkshedding', a form of freewriting that encourages reflection and animates discussion.[3] Students write in response to a prompt or a presentation, and the resulting texts are circulated and often end up in the students' journals. They might write about their evolving research plans, define key terms from the literature they are reading, describe problems or anxieties their work is causing, or otherwise use writing to put some shape to their thoughts. Some sample entries:

> [H]ow can I be expected to produce papers, conference talks and ideas, if I do not interrogate the complex and diverse composition of my individual identity, academic and otherwise, and have it reflected in my writing? I am therefore both surprised and refreshed that during this, perhaps my last university degree, I am being asked to *bring myself to the table,* as a means of establishing myself within an appropriate discourse community.
>
> (Journal entry)

> I think I can speak for most PhD students when I say that the stress of establishing a credible reputation in our respective discourse communities looms persistently in our thoughts. Adding to this stress is the importance of publishing to establish one's scholarly reputation, and conflicting opinions regarding the appropriate time for submitting, and how to determine your *readiness* for publication.
>
> (Journal entry)

> If I wrote poetry, I would be a poet. I would like to write this dissertation and still be a poet.
>
> (Journal entry)

> Entering the PhD without a consuming focus, what I hear some col-
> leagues refer to as a 'burning question,' and without funding so far,
> leaves me with the same feeling. I'm on a bus and I'm not quite sure yet
> where it's going. The scary part is, I'm the one driving the bus.
>
> (Journal entry)

> One of my goals throughout this doctoral journey is to produce
> [thoughtful], good, publishable writing. At the same time, I don't want
> to get swallowed by my self-induced obsession with productivity, to the
> extent that it cancels out my artistic drive.
>
> (Journal entry)

In addition, particularly during the student's first year, strategies and
resources for writing are explored – including the formation and maintenance of writing groups – and the collaborative dynamic between student
and supervisor and student and committee members is a frequent topic.
This latter subject is highly sensitive and critically important: the student–
supervisor relationship, though probably the most intimate and high-stakes
educational relationship of a student's life, is a seriously under-examined
and under-theorized teaching and learning situation (Kamler and Thomson,
2006). Aitchison and Lee (2006) have made effective use of writing groups
to create a sense of community among doctoral students and to distribute
the possibility of mentorship beyond the supervisory dyad.

Truth be told, the dissertation is a co-authored text, and the supervisor is
usually the invisible second author. What kind of feedback should students
expect and seek from supervisors? How might they make best use of their
time with supervisors? What should they do if they are at odds with supervisors, or feel they are not getting the feedback they require? Those of us
who have co-authored or co-edited know how much work it is to develop
fruitful and harmonious working relations around the production of texts,
and we also know how delicate those connections can be. As newcomers
to academic work, students need explicit assistance to help them develop
productive collaborative relations with their supervisors (and others). In
discussion, students had this to say about the supervisory relationship:

> And I want to stress that there was a real affinity, yeah. That's why I
> ended up choosing her as my supervisor. Yeah, there was an affinity. And
> I wonder how you work with someone with whom you don't have an
> affinity. And I do know people who do that and they cry a lot and they
> self-mutilate. It is just such an intimate, intense relationship. I had two
> other supervisors before I was with [my current supervisor], so I was
> really searching for someone who could help me in a particular way.
>
> (Focus group discussion)

[W]hat I have with my supervisor, and what I hear other people have, is there is a shared passion and engagement for the craft, for the process and the product and the unknown future. There is this kind of thrust towards the future and being valued for what you are now but also valued for what you could produce, what you can be. That for me is a part of a good apprenticeship where it is kind of like you join a guild because you want to do this thing that other people are doing in the best possible way. And I don't know how you gain that experience if you are with someone who is not valuing you as someone who is a potential colleague, a member of the guild. That's really tough. I need that affirmation.

(Focus group discussion)

Increasingly, over the two years, students are asked to raise the level of preparation and formality for their seminar presentations, beginning with conversations that grow out of inkshedding and developing to the type of 20-minute paper that is common at academic conferences. The writing that supports these presentations evolves from notes to full-scale academic arguments. In their second-year seminar, students circulate their comprehensive papers for critique and rehearse their oral comprehensive presentations. Outside the classroom, a number of activities complement the effort made in the seminars. Students are encouraged to present work-in-progress at regular public seminars, called Research Exchange Forums, at which faculty members also present, sometimes on panels with the students they are supervising. The graduate student society holds an annual academic conference, with a widely circulated call for papers, and again students are encouraged to participate; as a result, they may find themselves presenting with or to some of the same scholars they are reading in their courses. A student-organized initiative, called the ABCs of the PhD, runs workshops on writing grant proposals, conducting a literature review, looking for a job and other topics.

In addition to these many occasions on which students can use writing and speaking to help them define and redefine their ideas, the programme provides opportunities for students to reflect on the activity of writing in the production of disciplinary knowledge. The first-year reading list is heavy with texts about writing, and students are assigned writing-related readings in other courses as well (see Appendix 1 for a sample list). One of the required texts in the first-year seminar is Kamler and Thomson's *Helping Doctoral Students Write: Pedagogies for Supervision* (2006); the required texts in the writing course include Giltrow's *Academic Writing: Writing and Reading across the Disciplines* (2002) and Hyland's *Disciplinary Discourses: Social Interactions in Academic Writing* (2004). All three books are written by writing researchers and are among the few that provide thoroughly well-theorized accounts of writing in the academy.

The key message of the seminars is repeated again and again: you are in the process of joining a discourse community whose chief activity is writing and the knowledge-making that writing performs. The effect of that process on identity is also a frequent theme. What does it mean to join a community of scholars, and what are the implications of that membership? What is the intellectual and ideological relationship between the individual researcher-teacher and her far-flung colleagues? Students are immediately encouraged to begin considering the variety of communities whose interests overlap with their own (e.g. teachers, teacher educators, policy makers, curriculum designers, community organizers, researchers) and to explore the discourse forums of those communities (e.g. journals, books, websites, conferences, newsletters). The stated assumption is that students will end their studies as experts in some area of human thought and action, and will therefore be a welcome addition to some community. The question is, which community? Whose discourse echoes their own concerns? To whom and with whom do members of particular disciplinary collectives speak and write? Where and how would they like to make a contribution? What sort of person, with what sort of world view, will different doctoral paths lead them to? Whom do they want to hang around with when they're done?

To answer those questions, students embark on what might be called an anthropological investigation of discourse communities. One assignment, begun in the first-year seminar and expanded in the writing course, invites students to examine journals that address the issues and topics that interest them. They are encouraged to consider the text as an archaeologist might consider an ancient tool in order to gain insight into the object's use and value within a culture. What are the text's distinguishing features? What purpose does it seem to serve? Who reads it? Why? When? How? What do its separate sections do? Students also compare one journal over time and a variety of journals within a discipline. How has the journal evolved, and why? Is the practitioners' journal different from the researchers' journal and, if so, why? Another assignment narrows the analytic focus to the individual article. What are its distinguishing features? How are its arguments structured? What sources of information are used? What level and kind of language is used? And so on.[4]

In the second year of the programme, students focus on their comprehensive papers – usually two papers that report on the theories, prior research and methodologies that are likely to support the student's own research. The doctoral seminar sessions are dedicated, in part, to an examination of sample comprehensive papers and the formulation of the questions for the comprehensives. Senior doctoral students are invited to speak about their experience writing and defending the comprehensive papers, and faculty members are asked to speak about assigning and assessing papers. The questions are, again, explicitly about writing: What is the rhetorical purpose of a comprehensive paper? What do readers of the paper expect to see? What makes a good paper? How are papers structured, and why? What writing problems might students anticipate? Versions of the comprehensive papers become dissertation chapters.

The same rhetorical analysis is extended to conference papers and journal articles, and second-year students are encouraged to make conference presentations and to consider publication possibilities. One suggestion is that students turn a comprehensive paper, or part of a paper, into an article. Students who feel less advanced in their research are encouraged to write book reviews, newsletter articles, newspaper op-ed pieces, or other non-refereed texts. Again, examples of each genre are reviewed and their rhetorical situation analysed.

A programme such as this, which provides students with frequent informal and formal opportunities to write and speak, and encourages a close, critical attention to their disciplinary community and its discourse practices, goes a long way towards helping students publish before they graduate. But it depends on the ability of faculty members to make explicit the rules of the game, and to work closely with students as they struggle to master those rules. And it also depends on students having frequent opportunities to write and speak in threat-free contexts, where taking intellectual and rhetorical chances is encouraged, even celebrated, and students can grope towards greater understanding by using language as a tool for thinking. The rush to publish, as I have argued here, can subvert that possibility.

Appendix: Reading about writing

Bazerman, C. and Prior, P. (eds) (2004) *What Writing Does and How It Does It,* Mahwah, NJ: Lawrence Erlbaum and Associates.

Caffarella, R. S. and Barnett, B. G. (2000) 'Teaching Doctoral Students to Become Scholarly Writers: The Importance of Giving and Receiving Critiques', *Studies in Higher Education*, 25 (1), 39–51.

Clark, I. (2007) *Writing the Successful Thesis and Dissertation: Entering the Conversation,* Upper Saddle River, NJ: Prentice-Hall.

Geisler, C. (1994) *Academic Literacy and the Nature of Expertise: Reading, Writing, and Knowing in Academic Philosophy,* Hillsdale, NJ: Erlbaum.

Giltrow, J. (2002) *Academic Reading: Writing and Reading across the Disciplines,* 3rd edn, Peterborough, ON: Broadview Press.

Green, B. (2005) 'Unfinished Business: Subjectivity and Supervision', *Higher Education Research and Development,* 24 (2), 151–63.

Hyland, K. (2004) *Disciplinary Discourses: Social Interactions in Academic Writing,* Ann Arbor, MI: University of Michigan Press.

Kamler, B. and Thomson, P. (2004) 'Driven to Abstraction: Doctoral Supervision and Writing Pedagogies', *Teaching in Higher Education,* 9 (2), 195–208.

Kamler, B. and Thomson, P. (2006) *Helping Doctoral Students Write: Pedagogies for Supervision,* London: Routledge.

Lundell, D. B. and Beach, R. (2002) 'Dissertation Writers' Negotiations with Competing Activity Systems', in C. Bazerman and D. Russell (eds) *Writing Selves/*

Writing Societies: Research from Activity Perspective, Fort Collins, CO: The WAC Clearinghouse and Mind, Culture, and Activity, pp. 483–514. Available at http://wac.colostate.edu/books/selves_societies/

Prior, P. (1998) *Writing/Disciplinarity: A Sociohistoric Account of Literate Activity in the Academy*, Mahwah, NJ: Lawrence Erlbaum Associates.

Richardson, L. (2003) 'Writing: A Method of Inquiry', in N. K. Denzin and Y. S. Lincoln (eds) *The Sage Handbook of Qualitative Research*, Thousand Oaks, CA: Sage Publications, pp. 499–541.

Rose, M. and McClafferty, K. A. (2001) 'A Call for the Teaching of Writing in Graduate Education', *Educational Researcher*, 30 (2), 27–33.

Notes

1 Bakhtin (1984: 110) expresses a similar idea: 'Truth is not born nor is it to be found inside the head of an individual person, it is born between people collectively searching for truth, in the process of their dialogic interaction'.

2 There are at least three contemporary perspectives that push the notion of genre beyond its traditional but limited use in systems of textual taxonomy. They include, in addition to the rhetorical genre theory described here, the concept of genre as employed in Hallidayan systemic functional linguistics (e.g. Reid, 1987; Cope and Kalantzis, 1993) and Swales's (1990) use of genre in the field of English for specific purposes (ESP). See Hyon (1966) for a review.

3 See http://www.stthomasu.ca/~hunt/dialogic/whatshed.htm for a full explanation of the history and practice of inkshedding.

4 Two very useful tools in this sort of analysis is Bazerman and Prior's (2004) *What Writing Does and How It Does It*, and Giltrow's (2002) *Academic Writing* (see Appendix 1).

References

Aitchison, C. and Lee, A. (2006) 'Research Writing: Problems and Pedagogies', *Teaching in Higher Education*, 11 (3), 265–78.

Bakhtin, M. (1984) *Problems of Dostoevsky's Poetics* (trans. C. Emerson), Minneapolis: University of Minnesota Press.

Bazerman, C. (1988) *Shaping Written Knowledge: The Genre and Activity of the Experimental Article in Science*, Madison, WI: University of Wisconsin Press.

Bazerman, C. (in press) 'Writing and Cognitive Development: Beyond Writing to Learn', in C. Bazerman, D. Figueiredo and A. Bonini (eds) *Genre in a Changing World*, West Lafayette, IN: Parlor Press.

Bazerman, C. and Prior, P. (eds) (2004) *What Writing Does and How It Does It*, Mahwah, NJ: Lawrence Erlbaum and Associates.

Berkenkotter, C. and Huckin, T. (1995) *Genre Knowledge in Disciplinary Communication: Cognition/Culture/Power*, Hillsdale, NJ: Lawrence Erlbaum Associates.

Berkenkotter, C., Huckin, T. and Ackerman, J. (1988) 'Conventions, Conversations, and the Writer: Case Study of a Student in a Rhetoric PhD Program', *Research in the Teaching of English*, 22, 9–43.

Berlin, J. A. (1987) *Rhetoric and Reality: Writing Instruction in American Colleges, 1900–1985*, Carbondale, IL: Southern Illinois University Press.

Bitzer, L. (1968) 'The Rhetorical Situation', *Philosophy and Rhetoric*, 1 (1), 5–6.

Bizzell, P. (1992) *Academic Discourse and Critical Consciousness*, Pittsburgh: University of Pittsburgh Press.

Britton, J. (1980) 'Shaping at the Point of Utterance', in A. Freedman and I. Pringle (eds) *Re-inventing the Rhetorical Tradition*, Ottawa, ON: Canadian Council of Teachers of English, pp. 61–5.

Burke, K. (1941) *The Philosophy of Literary Form: Studies in Symbolic Action*, Berkeley: University of California Press.

Coe, R., Lingard, L. and Teslenko, T. (eds) (2002) *The Rhetoric and Ideology of Genre: Strategies for Stability and Change*, Cresskill, NJ: Hampton Press.

Cope, B. and Kalantzis, M. (eds) (1993) *The Powers of Literacy: A Genre Approach to Teaching Writing*, Bristol, PA: Falmer Press.

Dias, P., Freedman, A., Medway, P. and Paré, A. (1999) *Worlds Apart: Acting and Writing in Academic and Workplace Contexts*, Mahwah, NJ: Lawrence Erlbaum Associates.

Emig, J. (1977) 'Writing as a Mode of Learning', *College Composition and Communication*, 28 (2), 122–8.

Flower, L. S. and Hayes, J. R. (1980) 'The Cognition of Discovery: Defining a Rhetorical Problem', *College Composition and Communication*, 31 (1), 21–32.

Flower, L. S. and Hayes, J. R. (1981) 'A Cognitive Process Theory of Writing', *College English*, 44, 765–77.

Freedman, A. (1987) 'Learning to Write Again: Discipline-Specific Writing at University', *Carleton Papers in Applied Language Studies*, 4, 95–115.

Freedman, A. (1993) 'Show and Tell? The Role of Explicit Teaching in Learning New Genres', *Research in the Teaching of English*, 27, 222–51.

Freedman, A. and Medway, P. (eds) (1994) *Genre in the New Rhetoric*, London: Taylor & Francis.

Gage, J. (1986) 'Why Write?', in A. Petrosky and D. Bartholomae (eds) *The Teaching of Writing*, Chicago: National Society for the Study of Education, pp. 8–29.

Giltrow, J. (2002) *Academic Writing: Writing and Reading across the Disciplines*, 2nd and 3rd edns, Peterborough, ON: Broadview Press.

Green, B. (2005) 'Unfinished Business: Subjectivity and Supervision', *Higher Education Research and Development*, 24 (2), 151–63.

Hunt, R. A. (1993) 'Texts, Textoids and Utterances: Writing and Reading for Meaning, in and out of Classrooms', in S. B. Straw and D. Bogdan (eds) *Constructive Reading: Teaching beyond Communication*, Portsmouth, NH: Heinemann-Boynton/Cook, pp. 113–29.

Hyon, S. (1966) 'Genre in Three Traditions: Implications for ESL', *TESOL Quarterly*, 30 (4), 693–722.

Kamler, B. and Thomson, P. (2006) *Helping Doctoral Students Write: Pedagogies for Supervision*, London: Routledge.

McCarthy, L. P. (1987) 'A Stranger in Strange Lands: A College Student Writing across the Curriculum', *Research in the Teaching of English*, 21, 233–65.

MacKinnon, J. (1993) 'Becoming a Rhetor: Developing Writing Ability in a Mature, Writing-Intensive Organization', in R. Spilka (ed.) *Writing in the Workplace: New Research Perspectives*, Carbondale, IL: Southern Illinois University Press, pp. 41–55.

Miller, C. (1984) 'Genre as Social Action', *Quarterly Journal of Speech*, 70, 151–67.
Paré, A. (2002) 'Genre and Identity: Individuals, Institutions, and Ideology', in R. Coe, L. Lingard and T. Teslenko (eds) *The Rhetoric and Ideology of Genre: Strategies for Stability and Change*, Cresskill, NJ: Hampton Press, pp. 57–71.
Paré, A., Starke-Meyerring, D. and McAlpine, L. (in press) 'The Dissertation as Multi-genre: Many Readers, Many Readings', in C. Bazerman, D. Figueiredo and A. Bonini (eds) *Genre in a Changing World*, West Lafayette, IN: Parlor Press.
Parry, S. (1998) 'Disciplinary Discourse in Doctoral Theses', *Higher Education*, 36, 273–99.
Porter, J. (1992) *Audience and Rhetoric: An Archaeological Composition of the Discourse Community*, Englewood Cliffs, NJ: Prentice Hall.
Prior, P. (1998) *Writing/Disciplinarity: A Sociohistoric Account of Literate Activity in the Academy*, Mahwah, NJ: Lawrence Erlbaum Associates.
Reid, I. (ed.) (1987) *The Place of Genre in Learning: Current Debates*, Geelong, Vic.: Deakin University, Centre for Studies in Literacy Education.
Rose, M. and McClafferty, K. A. (2001) 'A Call for the Teaching of Writing in Graduate Education', *Educational Researcher*, 30 (2), 27–33.
Swales, J. (1990) *Genre Analysis*, Cambridge: Cambridge University Press.

Chapter 4

Dovetailing under impossible circumstances

Christine Pearson Casanave

I am deeply grateful to the people who helped me construct this chapter even when they had so little time and energy to do so. This chapter is about, and for, them.

Introduction

Being asked to contribute to this volume took me back to my own doctoral studies and made me reflect on the expectations that I had for myself then and that faculty had for me, about writing for publication before I had completed my degree. My situation was very different from that of the students I describe later in this chapter: I had no full-time job, only a teaching fellowship on campus; I had no family or children living with me; I had few health problems; I had, in other words, the luxury of studying just about full time (three-plus years of course work, three years of dissertation work, typical for an American university). However, unlike some of my colleagues from other US universities, I do not recall the faculty urging me to publish my work, even though I managed to get started on my own. Others have reported being urged to turn good course papers into articles to submit for publication or being self-motivated to do so (see, for example, Hedgcock, 2008; Lee and Norton, 2003; Matsuda, 2003).

Things have changed (or I was out of touch back then). In the broad field of second-language education, we seem to take it for granted now that (a) it is important to publish work from dissertations and (b) it is important not to wait to do this until we have diplomas in our hands. Publishing needs to start early if we are to compete in an increasingly tight job market. Employers, even in non-English-dominant institutions, are demanding evidence of publication (and often publication in English-language international journals with high "impact factors") as a basic requirement for employment or promotion (Curry and Lillis, 2004; Flowerdew, 1999, 2000; Lillis and Curry, 2006). Some universities as well are requiring that doctoral students publish in international journals as part of graduation requirements (see, for example, the case studies by Yongyan Li, in the field of science: Li, 2005, 2006a, 2006b, 2007; Li and Flowerdew, 2007).

Japan, the context for this chapter, is no exception. The expectation is increasing there, as elsewhere in Asia, that university job applications be accompanied by several published articles, especially for full-time positions, although a presentation of research and evidence of teaching may also be required. Some Japanese universities have also instituted a publication requirement for graduation from doctoral programs. Having several publications in hand by the time they graduate serves students well because many foreign (i.e. non-Japanese) and even Japanese teachers do not have secure full-time jobs. They are on the move, and on the lookout for better positions in a shrinking educational economy. More jobs are short-term contract positions, and even these ask for evidence of publications.

But, for now, I want to ask some questions about the pressures that students have to publish and state some of my hesitations at jumping on the publishing bandwagon. I won't claim, for instance, that all doctoral students need to publish while they are working on their dissertations. My hesitation surfaced after I had worked for several years in a doctoral program at the American university's Japan campus that I feature in this chapter. I had become increasingly astonished at the packed and pressured lives of most of my students, who still managed to work toward their doctoral degrees. Therefore, as part of my pedagogy of publishing, I ask students to examine their own situations carefully so they can make informed decisions about whether to try to publish, and, if so, what kinds of publishing to strive for given the realities of the publishing process. If students in a doctoral program wish to get some experience of publishing, without the risk and time involved in submitting work to international refereed journals, what intermediate steps can faculty and students take together as a way to dovetail course work, dissertation work, and publishing (and editing) experience within the realities of their lives? After looking at the "impossible circumstances" of some students, I describe one such project, a student-edited Working Papers publication, as one example of an intermediate step to publication.

The context of my discussion in this chapter is an applied linguistics graduate program at a branch campus of an American university in Japan, offering MA and EdD degrees. At the time I drafted this chapter, the program was about 25 years old, and had graduated approximately 100 students with a doctorate from the two branch campuses in Osaka and Tokyo. The founding director of the doctoral program had just been replaced, as had the dean of the university's Japan campus, but a new cohort had been admitted, so the program seemed secure for the time.

Graduate classes are given evenings and weekends to accommodate students' work schedules. Typical for US doctoral programs, students take courses (48 units, about two and a half years), pass qualifying examinations, and write and defend both a dissertation proposal and later a dissertation.

There is as yet no option to complete the doctorate with a coherent collection of publications instead of the dissertation. The time limit for finishing the doctorate without special extensions is seven years.

The program is very small in terms of staff, with a director who also teaches, and no permanent full-time faculty, as of 2008. The handful of part-time faculty have full-time jobs elsewhere. Guest lecturers offer weekend seminars several times a semester, but are not in residence and cannot do much dissertation advising. However, doctoral students sometimes work with a faculty member outside the university. There is a large number of students, with several cohorts of about 40–50 each (including Osaka and Tokyo campuses) in the pipeline. The students, a mix of Japanese (mostly female and some male) and non-Japanese (mostly male native English speakers, many married to Japanese, and a few female Koreans or Chinese), are a diverse group of mainly mid-career adults who work full time or the equivalent, and who make great personal and financial sacrifices to pursue their degrees. All work is done in English, with the exception of some students who might collect data and do some reading in Japanese or another non-English first language. All the Japanese students, and the few students from Korea and China, are thus undertaking the bulk of their doctoral work in a second language.

What I find remarkable is how many of the students juggle a crushing schedule of teaching (relentless work in many Japanese schools and universities) with studies and family life, to be described further below. Yet, in accordance with trends well discussed in this volume, pressure to publish during and shortly after doctoral study is increasing as a way to secure a job, to move up the ranks or get tenure, or to change jobs to something more desirable.

Impossible circumstances

Let me now sketch in general what I see as some of the impossibilities that challenge doctoral students in this program, making it difficult for them not only to think about writing for publication before they graduate but also just to get through the program. I believe that these challenges are not unique to students at this American university in Japan, but may reflect the realities of students elsewhere, particularly in schools of education, where students tend to be older, mid-career working teachers who have been in the field for a while. The challenges may also be more daunting for students in a US university, particularly those working in their second language, where years of course work precede dissertation research.

First is the need for all students but a fortunate few to work full time, often with added part-time courses, or to patch together several part-time jobs. In Japan, a full-time high school job can consume six and even seven days a week for 10–12 hours a day. University work tends to be much heavier than in North America, and may include many extra time-consuming duties. In addition to long work commutes, many students also have long commutes to and from the Tokyo or Osaka campuses for course work and consultations, sometimes requiring an overnight in a hotel. Unlike at the main campus in the US, there is no tuition aid for "foreign" students, nor are there any research and teaching fellowships.

Second, some students are burdened with crushing personal obligations. These include health problems related to stress, aging, or other infirmities; caring for aging parents or small children at home; and coping with exhaustion. A cynical joke has it that "incomplete" is the most popular grade in the program. When personal obligations and circumstances get in the way of completing the degree, it is often the degree that gets put on a back burner. Otherwise, the strains on family relationships and health are too great. Expecting such students to think about publishing during their course work and dissertation years, to conceptualize an audience beyond their five committee members, may not be realistic, as much as students would like to be able to do this.

Finally, contact between faculty and students, and even among students, is severely limited. The teaching staff are few and consumed with their full-time work elsewhere and so have little time to meet students or provide timely detailed feedback on work; students also have little choice as to who they work with (and few choices of courses to take). Students are on their own to form study groups and to find someone supportive to work with. The risk of not doing so is isolation.

All of this adds up to circumstances that I have labeled "impossible." In spite of these challenges, most doctoral students I have worked with show incredible commitment and tenacity to finish their degrees, and even to write for publication. Those who choose to postpone writing for publication do so for good reasons. In good conscience, I cannot push them more than I do. I can only suggest ways to dovetail.

The perspectives of students

At the time I drafted this chapter, I was working closely with approximately 15 doctoral students whom I knew from previous full-time work at the university. All were interested in qualitative inquiry for part or all of their dissertations. Most had finished course work and were working on dissertation proposals or writing dissertations. From my home base in California, I was employed as an adjunct in online independent studies and continued to work with 13 students in 2008. My own area of specialty is qualitative and narrative inquiry, and issues in academic writing, professional development, and writing for publication.

The stories I retell in this section were shared with me by 11 students, of whom seven were female (six Japanese, one UK) and four were male (one

Japanese and three North American). Their ages ranged from 40 to 55. Eight were married, eight had children, two were single, and one was divorced. Seven had full-time work (and most of these had additional part-time jobs), three had two or three part-time jobs at different universities, and one was not working. One of the students worked at a high school and the other working students taught at Japanese universities. They had all finished two to three years of course work, several were working on proposals, several others on finishing the dissertation, and one had graduated. They reported that they had enrolled in the doctoral program mainly to improve their job situations, but a number of them also commented that at mid-career they desired intellectual stimulation and challenge. Ten of the 11 had published something during their doctoral work, but not necessarily from the dissertation (e.g., articles about teaching, ESL/EFL textbooks). One student said that the new director discouraged publication from quantitative dissertation work before graduation because the work was supposed to be new.

I knew these students well, from having taught most of them in person in one or more courses and from official and unofficial online advising. In my official online advising, I asked students to stay in touch with me regularly, even if they had not been able to get much work done. Hence, email messages often contained personal information about what was holding them up. I thus became concretely aware of many of the constraints in students' lives. Then, for this chapter, I sent students specific questions about their lives and their experiences and views of publishing. This chapter, once drafted, was shared with them to check for accuracy and relevance, and to make sure that no confidential information was included. I made changes as needed. In the sections that follow, I offer some of their views in their own voices, and follow these with a description of the Working Papers project.

Work obligations and schedules; financial constraints

Nearly all the students in this particular doctoral program had work schedules that struck me as too demanding to allow them time or energy to work on dissertations and publishing. To give just a few examples, a middle-aged Japanese male, married with three children, wrote:

> I am a full-time professor at X University. This university is notorious for all the non-academic duties imposed on the teachers (e.g., weekly homeroom guidance, entrance examination committees, frequent open campus sessions, students' study trips, repeated, meaningless revision of curricula for no practical purposes, and a dozen other committee jobs). Also, in order to support my family, I must teach part-time at two other universities, and the class preparation takes up a huge amount of time.

One of the North American men, who had a wife and child at home, also had 12-hour days, including some Saturday mornings. "When I get home in the evenings," he said, "I am in no condition to do any serious concentrated work or study." He added that he "was only able to get through [the university's] course work by doing most of that work during the breaks between semesters." Another of the North Americans, a man with two small children at home, and numerous projects outside his doctoral program, said that he went "directly home after teaching and help[s] out with the kids until they are asleep – usually about 10 pm. Only then do I get to start my doctoral work."

A Japanese woman informed me that, even though she did not teach every day, she was required to be on her university campus five days a week, and had a long commute – two hours a day. She often spent 12 hours a day on campus, and was involved in many extra duties. Her fatigue was debilitating, and it had affected her health. Another Japanese woman had two small children, worked four days a week with a long commute, and still managed to drop off and pick up her children from child care. A British high school teacher wrote that five, sometimes six, days a week she "leave[s] home in the morning at 6:30 and get[s] home again in the evening at about 6:30." This woman has a husband and three children she also cares for.

Part-time teachers often teach many more classes than full-time teachers, but may not have to be on campus five days a week. A married Japanese woman, age 53, for instance, was teaching nine classes during the last year of her dissertation work, on four days. A fifth day was often taken up in doctor's visits for a serious health problem that caused her great fatigue, among other inconveniences. Another woman, trying to support herself and her two children as a divorcee, taught a total of 14 classes at three universities, requiring about 10 hours a week simply commuting. Her schedule filled five days a week, and left her only two afternoons for shopping and lesson preparation.

These schedules are not unique to the group of students who communicated with me for this chapter. Nearly all the students I talked to juggled full- and part-time work schedules with family life and health problems (described in more detail below).

Financial stresses do not help students sleep well. As I pointed out earlier, all Japanese students, and to my knowledge most non-Japanese except perhaps for a couple of American citizens, pay full tuition at this expensive American university. With some exceptions, they are supporting themselves or families, contributing to the support of aging parents, and trying to make ends meet in an expensive economy that has been in a recession since 1990.

Family situations; illness

Every student I got to know as part of my teaching over several years had pressing family situations, in addition to work pressures. Those women who were married and/or had children carried on with their traditional duties, including caring for parents or in-laws. Some of the men as well as women who had young children at home needed to support growing families financially and spend some time with their children in those precious early years. One Japanese woman with a full-time job and two small children said: "There are no limits, holidays, for child-raising. When I don't work, I take care of my kids. My dissertation doesn't complain. My kids do." Several single women appeared on the surface to have an easier situation. However, by age 50 these women were taking care of aging parents, including arranging for easing their mothers through the last stages of life. Six of my students, four single women and two married women, lost parents, in-laws, or other close relatives in the past year while they were trying to work on dissertations.

Many students, particularly women, told me of health problems that slowed down their progress greatly. One student, a single Japanese woman, aged 40, lived with her mother and did not work because she was so severely constrained by an insidious health problem that sometimes left her incapacitated for days at a time. Another student, a male from North America married to a Japanese and who had a young child, battled debilitating fatigue and mood swings that were only partially alleviated by medication. Several students suffered from painful back and neck problems. All of these students somehow managed little by little to move ahead on their dissertation work and even to present work at conferences and publish occasionally.

Need to publish before graduating

Not every student felt they could publish before graduating. One Japanese man who was already secure in his tenured job wanted to move into a more nourishing environment, and both the degree and publications would help him do that. However, he could not find a way to think about publishing yet, given his schedule. A North American man explained that "Right now, finishing the doctorate is what I want to concentrate on most." A Japanese woman also "prioritized finishing my dissertation." Nevertheless, she presented some of her dissertation work at an international conference, but did not write up the paper for publication at that time. Another woman began her study out of "academic curiosity" but felt increasingly pressured "to earn a doctorate for a secure post in the job market." She had published a couple of things, but finishing the degree was uppermost in her mind.

In contrast, two of the North American men felt strongly that they needed to publish before graduating. One had already published several pieces based on early dissertation work – pieces that had developed from course work. As one of the only respondents who was publishing work that he hoped would later evolve into his dissertation, he felt strongly that his publications "have been a help rather than a hindrance to my dissertation writing." The other North American man who was committed to publishing stated firmly: "I was so set on publishing when I entered the program that I don't recall if anyone encouraged me or not. It wouldn't have mattered – from the very beginning I felt it was crucial." This man had been inspired by an article on the topic of publishing while in graduate school (see Matsuda, 2003), and was persuaded that "graduate students should indeed write to publish as a matter of joining the professional community and building their knowledge base." With some regret, he admitted that he had not yet published anything from his early dissertation work, which was at the proposal development stage at the time of this writing.

Opinions were thus mixed on whether students felt they needed to publish something from the dissertation before graduating. Many said that ideally they would like to be able to do this, but that it did not seem possible at the time. Others said that the "sacrifices" required were worth it.

Deciding whether to publish

Given the impossible circumstances in which many of my students try to get dissertation work done, a number of them gave priority to finishing the dissertation first. But some students had already published other kinds of pieces such as EFL textbooks or teaching practice pieces, singly or co-authored, and a couple had published early dissertation work.

For example, two Japanese women had prepared articles from early dissertation ideas for a refereed journal within Japan, one taking two years to finish her article. She noted that "The reviewers' comments on the original manuscript were very useful. The publishing process taught me a lot about what publishing on academic journals is like, and prepared me to some extent for the dissertation process." The other took "three years and eight months from start to finish," explaining that she revised "again and again," and "re-re-re-submitted" her paper, asking for help from colleagues, friends, and professors, until it was finally accepted. This experience, she said, was a "great opportunity . . . on how to be socialized into the academic world." But the process may have been unnecessarily difficult, because she "did not have the schema for publication and did not figure out what I should do or what would happen next." An intermediate publishing experience might have helped her in this regard. A third student, one of the North American men, worked on a book chapter from his dissertation ideas over a period of several years, grateful for the difficult but rewarding experience. In spite of the lengthy process, all the students who had published in refereed journals or books reported on the benefits to them of learning about the review and revision processes. Their work improved, and they came to learn at first hand about how long it takes to get a piece of work in print.

In sum, all the students who corresponded with me spoke of the importance of publishing, and of their desires to do so before they graduated, circumstances permitting. But, as is clear from their stories, circumstances did not always permit, particularly if students wanted to publish dissertation-related work in refereed journals.

Dovetailing

By dovetailing, I refer to strategies of combining efforts and resources so that these are not duplicated needlessly. Reading, class work, thinking, and work on dissertations can be merged to some extent, as is the case when faculty encourage students to make connections among class work, dissertations, and future publications rather than see their work as fragmented and unrelated to dissertation and publication. With faculty support and student interest, much of students' course work can provide a background for dissertation work, and be compiled into an "intermediate" publication, several types of which were available at this university. I describe two of these briefly, then expand on one that I participated in, the Working Papers collection. The approaches I mention below are quite different from those in which students are offered specific classes in ESP (English for special purposes) or EAP (English for academic purposes) disciplinary writing (e.g. Dressen-Hammouda, 2008; Swales and Feak, 2000; Swales and Lindemann, 2002; see also chapters in Johns, 2002, and Flowerdew and Peacock, 2001). There were no such doctoral classes at this university, much to the regret of some students. Rather, I am talking about intermediate practices, between class work and the professional activity of publishing. (For a view of mentoring that is compatible with this practice-participatory approach, see Simpson and Matsuda, 2008; see also some of the tales in Casanave and Vandrick, 2003, and Casanave and Li, 2008.)

Applied linguistics series and colloquia proceedings

Students at the Graduate College of Education at this university occasionally compiled papers on particular topics in applied linguistics. Beginning in 1984, with a faculty member as one of the editors and with the support of the director, papers by students on teaching methods and materials were collected and edited by a student committee, copied and bound in-house, and stored in the College of Education office. A more elaborate intermediate step to publishing was this university's Applied Linguistics Colloquium, an annual event begun in the late 1990s, organized by a volunteer faculty member, supported by the director, and staffed by alumni and students. The Colloquium sends a call for papers to all students and alumni, and also to the main foreign-language teaching organization in Japan. Participation is thus competitive and simulates higher-risk professional events. A number of the students I talked to had shared their research in this forum and published it later in the Colloquium Proceedings. Participating in the Colloquium and the Proceedings is especially useful for students who are in the midst of dissertation work. The Proceedings is sponsored by a faculty member, and edited in part by volunteers who have already graduated or are still in the program. Like the applied linguistics series, the Colloquium Proceedings are copied and stored in-house. It is not clear how widely read they are beyond the in-house audience.

Student-edited Working Papers from course writings: ideal dovetailing

A low-risk intermediate project on the path to publishing, especially useful for students who have never published before, is the Working Papers collection. On three occasions, twice for a doctoral class and once for a master's class, I suggested to students that they revise and compile course writings into a Working Papers collection, to be edited by a student committee, guided by me where necessary, and copied and bound at the university's expense. The previous director supported these projects, and there was a collection of these Working Papers from past years on file, along with collections of the other in-house publications. To my knowledge, the Working Papers, like the Colloquium Proceedings, has a small readership of current and past students at the university.

What distinguished the Working Papers collections that I participated in from the Applied Linguistics series or the Colloquium Proceedings was the following: The papers did not have to be in any sense "finished" – we took the "Working Papers" title seriously and envisioned the papers as a step to something else; I did not take a role as co-editor or organizer (beyond getting people started); with a couple of exceptions, the papers were limited to those that originated in my own class; and the student authors and editors worked together over time to revise the submissions.

Getting started

Each time we have done a Working Papers collection, the project came into being only at the end of the semester. I have not begun my classes announcing to students that we will do this, concerned that their writing and thinking might be constrained by concerns about "going public." Much later in the course, I have encouraged students to consider a Working Papers project if I found the course writings (e.g., reading response journals, final course papers) especially interesting and worth sharing with others, and if the writings might help move students' larger projects forward in some way. Several weeks before the end of a term, I described my idea, assured everyone that there was absolutely no requirement for anyone to submit anything, and informed everyone of the time obligations, given that it was not a simple matter of photocopying and binding "as-is" course papers. I let them know that continuing to work on one or more course writings for the purpose of including it in an edited collection could be a valuable learning experience: seeing course writings as a step to something more; receiving comments from peer editors and doing the necessary revising and polishing; being able to add an item to their CVs. All this could happen with essentially no risk, so it was ideal for novice scholarly writers. I then asked for several volunteer editors and met with them to discuss logistics and timing.

Timing

One of the main frustrations with the Working Papers edited collection is how long it can take to see the collection in its finished form. The three collections that I have helped students compile took from a year to two years to complete. (Given the realities of students' lives, deadlines need to be flexible.) I consider this one of the many realistic aspects of publishing, and must make sure that I prepare students for it. Both student authors and editors need to be around, or to stay in touch, during the entire process. Moreover, a faculty member who sets such a project in motion needs to be around in one form or another (in my case, it turned out to be online) to follow through to the conclusion of the project, guide and trouble-shoot as needed, and send encouraging words.

Types of papers

It might seem like common sense for students to submit only, or mainly, pilot research papers for a Working Papers edited collection. This is certainly one type of course paper that students have revised for a collection, and that dovetails nicely with evolving thesis and dissertation work. However, many students that I have worked with are at quite early stages of masters or doctoral work. In the case of my doctoral students, the courses I have taught in qualitative inquiry were intended to immerse students in readings of issues, conceptual frameworks, and strategies for inquiry. The goal of such courses was to help students locate themselves in a tradition of inquiry and to do readings that would feed into future work so that they can discuss research concepts, assumptions, and traditions knowledgeably rather than as mere technicians who can use certain research skills. Hence important kinds of writing that can be revised for a collection are reading response journals, conceptual papers, or literature reviews.

My role during the term

My aims in my graduate courses have been to introduce students to important readings, to use writing and discussion to help them think through issues and assumptions underlying inquiry traditions, and to help them develop topics and research designs for their own inquiry. To these ends, students wrote response journals or research memos (Maxwell, 2004) approximately every two weeks, to which I responded in writing as promptly as I could. If there was a final course paper, I also responded in some detail as promptly as I could. Students submitted work to me electronically and I responded using the "comment" and "track changes" functions. Students could use these comments to revise a selection of their written work for the collection if they chose to submit something. When time permitted, I also asked students to read and comment on each other's response journals. The ongoing interaction parallels the interactions that published writers engage in as they prepare drafts for publication, in contrast to much course work writing that students do in relative isolation from colleagues and mentors, and sometimes with little feedback from professors.

Responsibilities of student authors

Not all students have chosen to submit one or more writings to a Working Papers collection. Such a project should never be required, and, for students who have already published, it may not benefit them greatly. Those who participate need to see the project as something that goes beyond course work and that will benefit their future work.

Students first need to decide whether they will submit something to the Working Papers collection, but to do so without feeling pressure from me or from peers. If they choose to submit something, they should consider which writings will contribute to furthering their work beyond the particular class we had together: Will it help them identify and articulate a research tradition? Understand assumptions underlying various methods? Synthesize and critique various readings? Doctoral students who have begun dissertation work benefit greatly from dovetailing their course writings with their evolving dissertation ideas and then attempting to articulate their ideas publicly.

The authors then need to be willing to revise, to negotiate, and to do their best to adhere to the schedule set by the editors. All authors should understand that their work will not be rejected – fear of rejection is not part of the process. However, they also should understand that their work will probably not be accepted "as is." Many novice scholars are shocked and discouraged at the time-consuming review-and-revise process of publishing.

The authors also need to decide how to represent themselves in their public writing, both in terms of writing style and voice, and in the form of a bio-statement. How personal or distant do they want to be? With students who are interested in qualitative inquiry, I encourage active voice and a more personal tone, a style that many students falsely believe they should avoid. I also have asked students to experiment with different bio-statements and to evaluate the effects of statements written in the first person as well as the third person. The authors and editors together decide how bio-statements will be written for the collection.

Responsibilities of student editors

To put together a Working Papers collection, three or four student editors volunteer to work on the project. Often, one or more of the editors has had some editorial experience before, either on a different departmental collection or on a language teacher association publication. These editors scaffold the editing experience for the newcomers. The editors have many more tasks to complete than do the authors, and they themselves also submit pieces for the collection.

First, the volunteer editors need to foresee that they will have time and energy to work on the collection for a year or more. I have shared tales of my own editing work, and tried to convince them that the task of editing does not involve compiling course papers. Rather, it requires that the student editors examine carefully the papers that classmates (and they) have submitted, and do the tedious work of actually editing, organizing, and formatting a real collection.

Early in the process, the editors need to construct a way to communicate regularly with all the student authors who decide to submit papers, to decide if each editor will be assigned particular people to work with, and to distribute the work of reading, reviewing, and communicating. They need also to set a schedule for when they hope to receive first, second, third (etc.) drafts, and to keep after their classmates in a way that will not cause distress to anyone. Importantly, the editors need to be willing to suggest changes to their classmates' work, and to do this in a way that is supportive.

Later, the editors need to organize a coherent edited volume (possibly by thematic sections) once they have received drafts from all authors, and to decide how to format it. They need then to prepare a final copy, with title page, preface, and table of contents, carefully proofreading everything, and checking that citation and referencing conventions have been followed. They need as well to arrange with the program director for getting the collection photocopied and distributed in print to cohort members and electronically as appropriate (very few print copies are made because of expense).

In short, the amount of extra work involved for the student writers, but especially for the editors, is significant, and all three cases that I was involved in stretched out over a year or more. The experience, however, for all who have written and edited for these in-house projects has been invaluable.

Reflections on the Working Papers project

The advantages of involving students in projects like this are many. First, the in-house editing and publishing experiences are real but low risk; second, they are generally more time-efficient than publishing in a refereed journal; and, third, they are a wonderful way to help students practice the conventions of academic writing including citation, and referencing, as well as the social and political negotiations needed to polish a piece for publication.

Moreover, the student editors learn a great deal about reviewing and editing the work of others, lessons they can also apply to themselves. We can consider such a project an intermediate step in helping students learn about publishing, because it falls between course papers and pieces for domestic and international journals. As one student said: "This [project] seemed to bring the impossible within reach."

As I was drafting this chapter, I was sent two such publications compiled by students, one from a master's class on second language writing and the other from a doctoral class on issues in qualitative inquiry. The latter was a 125-page PDF draft of papers from revised reading response journals, put together by three student editors (one of whom contributed his ideas to this chapter), from work by students in a doctoral class from 2006. The students in this group were starting to think about dissertation proposals and trying to locate themselves in a tradition of inquiry. About half of the students in the class contributed papers to the collection. Some had published before, and some had not. The editing process took two years of intermittent work.

The doctoral collection that developed from the reading response journals reflects a good attempt at what I have called dovetailing. Students initially do no extra work beyond that required for their courses. Those who want to do so continue working, bit by bit, to prepare a version for the in-house collection. This kind of dovetailing requires extra work not only by the student authors and editors, but also by the faculty sponsor, who needs a sincere commitment to the value of this kind of effort in helping students get their foot in the door of publishing. I do not recommend it for faculty who themselves do not have time or like to write for publication, to edit, or to guide students in their writing. I happen to like these activities, and above all I like to see what happens to students' confidence and vision for their work once they begin to see that it can go beyond their course work, and eventually, beyond their dissertations, into the public arena.

Let me conclude by reiterating why I do not ask all students to write course papers to submit for publication in refereed journals rather than in a Working Papers collection, other than perhaps to use such papers as a starting point. First, some students do not need or want to do this, or perhaps, because of the constraints in their lives such as those discussed in this chapter, they would not be able to do this even if they wanted to. I ask students merely to consider dovetailing course papers with conference presentations and possible publications if they are motivated to do so, as do other faculty members in this program.

Second, I believe it is the rare person, including experienced published writers, who can write a draft of an article for publication in a 14-week semester. I once tried writing along with some students at a different university where I was working, and could not finish my 10-page draft to my satisfaction. Moreover, the entire process of getting that small paper published took three years. It is not fair to convey the idea to students that writing and publishing can happen quickly, given the drafting, revising, reviewing, and further revising that are essential. Although I have no hard evidence for this view, in my capacity as a member of several journal editorial boards, I sense that some novice authors submit manuscripts prematurely, naively believing either that the work is adequate or that reviewers and editors will edit the work for them. The result can be a discouraging rejection or review process for students, including the belief by some users of English as a second language that they have been discriminated against (see Flowerdew, 2008, and the response by Casanave, 2008).

Third, at the proposal or dissertation writing stage, students who submit articles for possible publication in refereed journals risk being distracted from their dissertation work, even when an article stems from this work, as a number of students commented in their correspondence with me. Students who are well within their time limits for finishing dissertations can afford to be sidetracked in this admittedly very rewarding way. However, those who are pressed for time or in other ways constrained by the realities of their lives may need to rethink their priorities. Although the publications stand them in good stead once done, with the deadlines imposed by editors, school work can get postponed unless the publication truly dovetails with dissertation work. In such cases of ideal dovetailing, students would be wise to check with their programs about whether (sections of) a published article can be used in a dissertation.

Final thoughts

My point in this chapter is that we should be doing everything we can to encourage and support students' efforts at publishing before they complete the dissertation, but that we need as well to attend closely to the realities of students' lives. I know that in my own case, unless I ask, or have ongoing communication with students, I don't know what is going on in their lives, and assume that they can forge ahead, concentrating on their dissertation work and publishing efforts as though these efforts were the center of their lives. Faculty staff seldom learn about the details of students' personal lives, to the detriment of all of us.

Understanding the realities of students' lives, we can identify numerous ways that novice or periphery scholars, in graduate programs or recently graduated, can become participants in actual professional practices such as publishing and presenting work in international venues. From the periphery in Sri Lanka, Canagarajah (2003) noted some "somewhat legitimate" discursive and textual strategies that periphery scholars, even experienced ones, used to negotiate their work into international publications. At the graduate student level, Simpson and Matsuda (2008) described mentor–mentee partnerships in which doctoral students participated in activities such as working on edited collections by the mentor and helping prepare conferences. In my own case, student-edited Working Papers represent such an intermediate step between course work and full participation in scholarly publishing in refereed journals. It is likely that even students whose impossible circumstances hinder them from attempting to publish in international journals can still move their publishing efforts forward by participating in a Working Papers project. It *is* possible to dovetail under impossible circumstances.

References

Canagarajah, A. S. (2003) 'A Somewhat Legitimate and Very Peripheral Participation', in C. P. Casanave and S. Vandrick (eds) *Writing for Scholarly Publication: Behind the Scenes in Language Education*, Mahwah, NJ: Lawrence Erlbaum Associates, pp. 197–210.

Casanave, C. P. (2008) 'The Stigmatizing Effect of Goffman's Stigma Label: A Response to John Flowerdew', *Journal of English for Academic Purposes*, 7 (4), 264–7.

Casanave, C. P. and Vandrick, S. (eds) (2003) *Writing for Scholarly Publication: Behind the Scenes in Language Education*, Mahwah, NJ: Lawrence Erlbaum Associates.

Casanave, C. P. and Xiaomina, L. (eds) (2008) *Learning the Literacy Practices of Graduate School: Insiders' Reflections on Academic Enculturation*. Ann Arbor: University of Michigan Press.

Curry, M. J. and Lillis, T. (2004) 'Multilingual Scholars and the Imperative to Publish in English: Negotiating Interests, Demands, and Rewards', *TESOL Quarterly*, 38 (4), 663–88.

Dressen-Hammouda, D. (2008) 'From Novice to Disciplinary Expert: Disciplinary Identity and Genre Mastery', *English for Specific Purposes*, 27 (2), 233–52.

Flowerdew, J. (1999) 'Writing for Scholarly Publication in English: The Case of Hong Kong', *Journal of Second Language Writing*, 8, 123–45.

Flowerdew, J. (2000) 'Discourse Community, Legitimate Peripheral Participation, and the Non-Native-English-Speaking Scholar', *TESOL Quarterly*, 34 (1), 127–50.

Flowerdew, J. (2008) 'Scholarly Writers who Use English as an Additional Language: What Can Goffman's "Stigma" Tell Us?', *Journal of English for Academic Purposes*, 7 (2), 77–86.

Flowerdew, J. and Peacock, M. (eds) (2001) *Research Perspectives on English for Academic Purposes*, Cambridge: Cambridge University Press.

Hedgcock, J. S. (2008) 'Lessons I Must Have Missed: Implicit Literacy Practices in Graduate Education', in C. P. Casanave and X. Li (eds) *Learning the Literacy Practices of Graduate School: Insiders' Reflections on Academic Enculturation*, Ann Arbor: University of Michigan Press, pp. 32–45.

Johns, A. M. (ed.) (2002) *Genre in the Classroom: Multiple Perspectives*, Mahwah, NJ: Lawrence Erlbaum Associates.

Lee, E. and Norton, B. (2003) 'Demystifying Publishing: A Collaborative Exchange between Graduate Student and Supervisor', in C. P. Casanave and S. Vandrick (eds) *Writing for Scholarly Publication: Behind the Scenes in Language Education*, Mahwah, NJ: Lawrence Erlbaum Associates, pp. 17–38.

Li, Y. (2005) 'Multidimensional Enculturation: The Case Study of an EFL Chinese Doctoral Student', *Journal of Asian Pacific Communication*, 15 (1), 153–70.

Li, Y. (2006a) 'A Doctoral Student of Physics Writing for International Publication: A Sociopolitically-Oriented Case Study', *English for Specific Purposes*, 25, 456–78.

Li, Y. (2006b) 'Negotiating Knowledge Contribution to Multiple Discourse Communities: A Doctoral Student of Computer Science Writing For Publication', *Journal of Second Language Writing*, 15, 159–78.

Li, Y. (2007) 'Apprentice Scholarly Writing in a Community of Practice: An Intraview of an NNES Graduate Student Writing a Research Article', *TESOL Quarterly*, 41 (1), 55–79.

Li, Y. and Flowerdew, J. (2007) 'Shaping Chinese Novice Scientists' Manuscripts for Publication', *Journal of Second Language Writing*, 16 (2), 100–17.

Lillis, T. and Curry, M. J. (2006) 'Professional Academic Writing by Multilingual Scholars: Interactions with Literacy Brokers in the Production of English-Medium Texts', *Written Communication*, 23 (1), 3–35.

Matsuda, P. K. (2003) 'Coming to Voice: Publishing as a Graduate Student', in C. P. Casanave and S. Vandrick (eds) *Writing for Scholarly Publication: Behind the Scenes in Language Education*, Mahwah, NJ: Lawrence Erlbaum Associates, pp. 39–51.

Maxwell, J. A. (2004) *Qualitative Research Design: An Interactive Approach*, 2nd edn, Thousand Oaks, CA: Sage Publications.

Simpson, S. and Matsuda, P. K. (2008) 'Mentoring as a Long-Term Relationship: Situated Learning in a Doctoral Program', in C. P. Casanave and S. Vandrick (eds) *Writing for Scholarly Publication: Behind the Scenes in Language Education*, Mahwah, NJ: Lawrence Erlbaum Associates, pp. 90–104.

Swales, J. M. and Feak, C. B. (2000) *English in Today's Research World: A Writing Guide*, Ann Arbor: University of Michigan Press.

Swales, J. M. and Lindemann, S. (2002) 'Teaching the Literature Review to International Graduate Students,' in A. M. Johns, (ed.) *Genre in the Classroom: Multiple Perspectives*, Mahwah, NJ: Lawrence Erlbaum Associates, pp. 105–19.

Chapter 5

Revise and resubmit

The role of publication brokers

Barbara Kamler

'Revise and resubmit.' These words can be simultaneously elating and terrifying for early career researchers. They carry both good news and bad news. The good news is that the article submitted for peer review is deemed to be acceptable. The journal wants the researcher's work and wishes to 'make public' their scholarship. Heady stuff for newcomers, this legitimizing and acknowledging that what they have argued and documented for critical academics in their field is okay. More than okay.

The bad news is that the submitted article is not acceptable in its current form. There is more work to be done. Before it is 'publishable' there needs to be revising, rethinking and redoing. 'Revise and resubmit' makes great demands on writers. It says the text does not quite do the job *yet*. Reviewers may offer advice about problems, omissions, infelicities of structure or phrase; they may raise methodological issues, citation queries or complain that the argument remains inexplicit. The truth is that very few writers welcome such news – even the most experienced – even when it is understood as a normal part of the journal review process.

I have been known to behave badly on first reading an editor's revise and resubmit letter and throw it across my study. Or lie down until I can figure out what it means and how I can find the time and energy to re-enter what I'd hoped was a finished text. But enter I must and often I seek help from colleagues to figure out what to do, despite my 25-plus years as a well-published writer.

Writing any article involves difficult structural and textual decisions about the most effective way to argue a case. So being asked to unstitch the garment that took so long to design and make in the first place is never warming news. We must find spaces in the text to insert more information without losing overall coherence. We need to use an economy of language to meet reviewer demands, but still stay within word limit. We need to decide which reviewer commentary to attend to closely and which to background. This is very difficult labour indeed.

In this chapter I focus on how to best support early career writers through the complexities of the revise and resubmit process. I write from my position as advocate of inexperienced doctoral and early career researchers who seek to publish their research in peer review journals. I have recently retired from a full-time university position to do consultancy work on academic writing and publishing in universities across Australia. Everywhere I go I find confusion and despair about articles rejected or returned for further work. In the face of negative commentary, too many inexperienced writers crumble and never resubmit. Some take the critique so personally that they are incapacitated. Others are unable to interpret what they are being asked to do. And too many negotiate the process without expert guides or adequate pedagogical resources.

So, I approach this chapter not as a neutral exponent of a publishing pedagogy but entangled in the lives and futures of emerging generations of academics. My work with Pat Thomson (Kamler and Thomson, 2006; Thomson and Kamler, 2009) on the enmeshed nature of text work and identity work makes me worry about the consequences of not conceptualizing the emotionality and also the potentially devastating effects of reviewer critique. I focus in particular on the revise and resubmit process because so little pedagogical attention has been paid to this aspect of the publishing regime – to what happens *after* the article is submitted. I argue strenuously that early career researchers must not be left to their own devices in learning how to navigate this difficult terrain.

To make my case, I call on the stories, reviewer reports, and letters to and from editors shared by generous academic writers – from the most to the least experienced. Additionally, I conducted three interviews with editors of high-ranking peer review journals in the social sciences to access their thoughts on the pedagogical role of editors. In all cases I use pseudonyms to anonymize the data source. The chapter begins with a brief discussion of the literature available on revise and resubmit and considers conceptual resources that might underpin a publishing pedagogy. I then use a number of case studies to explore two practices I have been developing: reading reviewer reports as text and writing to editors to document the revisions made. I conclude by arguing for a broader commitment to publication brokering in any pedagogy that helps novice researchers become robust participants in how the publication game is played and won.

Moving from procedure towards pedagogy

In surveying the kinds of literature available on the revise and resubmit process, it becomes clear that much of it is embedded in academic writing handbooks and guides for students, where it consists of a section or chapter, often framed as advice.

Elsewhere I have written with Pat Thomson (Kamler and Thomson, 2008) of the dangers and limitations of the advice genre so prevalent in doctoral education; of our preference for texts that recognize the knowledge and agency of doctoral researchers and offer them an intelligent set of resources for making difficult textual decisions. In this regard, some of the most useful texts I've found on 'revise and resubmit' are those that give students a feel for the complexities and politics of journal peer review, rather than simply treating the process procedurally or neutrally.

Murray (2005), for example, in *Writing for Academic Journals,* offers actual reviewer comments – showing both destructive and encouraging feedback – as well outlining common reasons for papers being rejected and how to deal with hostile reviews. Wellington (2003), in *Getting Published: A Guide for Lecturers and Researchers*, does similar work in making explicit the kinds of critical commentary authors can expect from reviewers. However, he also asks: why do we subject people to peer review? His interviews with 12 editors of education journals illuminate the editor's perspective on peer review and bring students into contested conversations about the drawbacks as well as the benefits of the system. Most interesting for newcomers is advice offered by Hartley (2008) in his book *Academic Writing and Publishing: A Practical Handbook.* The following exhortation to reviewers signals dissatisfaction with what might be called ungenerous reviewing practices:

- Be courteous throughout. There is no need to be superior, sarcastic or to show off. Remember the paper you are refereeing might have been written by a postgraduate, and it could be a first attempt at publication.
- Avoid criticising the paper because it does not do what you might have done. Judge it on its own merits.
- Explain any criticisms that you make. There must always be a reason for them.

(Hartley, 2008: 154–5)

A somewhat different approach is offered through case studies in Casanave and Vandrick's (2003) *Writing for Scholarly Publication: Behind the Scenes in Language Education.* A number of chapters in this edited collection foreground the graduate student perspective by documenting their struggles to get published, to find voice and negotiate power and position in particular academic communities. A particularly powerful account by Kubota (2003) examines her anxieties and confusions when, after receiving two reviewer reports that recommended rejection, she was subsequently invited by the editor to resubmit her article. Negotiating the process with the assistance of a trusted, experienced colleague proved essential to her eventual publication success.

Taken together, such texts offer valuable information to publishing novices. They make visible key textual components of the process and provide insights into the genres and debates that surround the practices of peer review. What they do not do, however, is explicitly address issues of pedagogy or develop mediation strategies to sustain aspiring writers. In this chapter I attempt such a move by working with the concept of publication brokering as a discursive social practice. My aim is to imagine new ways of working with early career writers *after* their articles have been reviewed and returned to them, so they might learn to manage the social, political and textual dimensions of the resubmission process.

Publication brokering as discursive social practice

Recent theorizing on the central role of expert guides in facilitating publication success comes from Lillis and Curry's (2006) work with multilingual scholars seeking publication in international peer review English-medium journals. They use the term 'literacy brokers' to designate those people – such as editors, reviewers, academic professionals, linguistic professionals, English-speaking friends and colleagues – who mediate text production in a variety of ways. Their text-oriented ethnographic research explores the impact of literacy brokering on scholars working outside English-speaking countries – from early drafts through to publication, from submission to resubmission.

Of particular interest is their notion that such brokering activity is not only a legitimate (rather than remedial) activity, but a form of mediation that makes a crucial difference to publication outcomes. Access to brokers is, Lillis and Curry (2006: 13) argue, a form of cultural capital that can enhance the prestige and reputation of writers and also secure more direct forms of economic gain, such as promotion and salary bonuses. Conversations with brokers about the specific content of an article, as well as broader disciplinary conversations and target journal conversations, play a crucial role in the successful publication of novice scholar texts.

I want to take up their argument here by using the term 'publication brokering' to mark the essential pedagogical work carried out by supervisors, writing groups and other academic professionals in mediating reviewer commentary. It is never simply a matter of students attending to what reviewers say and then addressing their concerns. Complex and difficult decisions need to be made about content, disciplinary knowledge, debates, structural framing and the discourses of the target journal. Kubota (2003: 68) captures the dilemma for novice journal writers when she advises them to:

> Be open to criticism from reviewers and editors. Receiving criticisms is often intimidating, but learning to accept them and align yourself with existing academic discourses are keys to professional success. At the same time, do not adhere slavishly to the suggestions given by reviewers. Too much preoccupation with following their suggestions can spoil the focus and coherence of your paper. At a certain point it may be wiser

to look for a better home for the paper than to keep trying to meet the demands of the reviewers or editors.

Access to brokers should not simply be serendipitous or available only to the privileged or to those brave enough to ask for assistance. A variety of players can take up this pedagogical brokering role, including journal reviewers who write informative and helpful reviews (not always the case); and editors who give useful guidance about how to traverse conflicting reviewer reports (not always the case). Certainly supervisors, trusted colleagues and peer writing groups of the kind described by Aitchison in Chapter 6 can provide critical distance and talk strategy about what action to take, while still keeping the argument and coherence of the article in the writer's control.

I understand this brokering work as a complex discursive social practice, which mediates the more immediate social contexts of the target journal and the broader disciplinary and political contexts of journal production itself. Like Thomson *et al.*, who in Chapter 9 (see also Kamler and Thomson 2006) mobilize a social discursive framework to explore a journal editing pedagogy, I want to tease out the layers of pedagogic activity involved in mediating the review process. Clearly newcomers find the resubmission process complex, troublesome and difficult to interpret. My question is: how can publication brokers help them interpret what is happening in the social, cultural and political climate of revise and resubmit so that they can take effective textual action? In the remainder of this chapter I discuss two pedagogic strategies that aim to do this work and diffuse the emotional response to receipt of reviewer comments.

Reading reviewer reports as text

Harsh rejections are unpleasant. Negative critique is often difficult to separate from the writer's self. It seems to take no time at all for wounded writers to generalize from poor article to defective writer to hopeless academic, when objectively all the reviewer text is authorized to say is that the article, or parts of it, does not work. This is an obvious but crucial point for publication brokers to emphasize and one that often escapes the emotional or exasperated writer.

A key move then for publication brokers is to read the reviewer commentary discursively *as text*, as a representation of reviewer opinion, not as the truth. Many experienced academics do this when they make public their own letters of rejection and critique, either in individual supervision sessions or in graduate writing seminars. The making public has the effect of building a writing community in which membership in the 'negative review club' is legitimized; in which difficult review stories become data for analysis, critique, joint problem-solving and action, not just for distress or complaint.

Here I want to explore the kind of brokering practices that create analytic distance on reviewer reports. I do this by developing case studies on Rajee, a full-time doctoral student in aeronautical engineering, and Sam, a part-time doctoral student in education (both pseudonyms). Both Rajee and Sam wanted to have their conference papers published in peer review journals and clearly benefited from the guidance of a more expert publication broker.

Rajee's story suggests that not all reviewer commentary is useful or specific enough to guide action. Rajee submitted her paper to an international aeronautical sciences conference documenting a new application of software she had developed to optimize lighter production of aircraft wing structure. For the paper, she devised a hypothetical use of the new software, as she was prohibited from releasing the detail of her techniques for reasons of commercial confidentiality until the thesis research was complete.

One review offered nine words: 'Very little contribution. Too many words, very limited results.' The other was more considerate and indicated that the 'technical content of the paper is original'. But its key criticism was that the paper was not 'complete and comprehensive' enough because it withheld the specificity of application she could not reveal: 'too much information is not substantiated due to confidentiality reasons.' The editor wanted her paper, but offered no way out of this confidentiality catch-22.

Rajee brought the paper to a publishing workshop I conducted at her university to problem-solve how she might revise and resubmit. I am no aeronautical engineering expert, I assure you, so I read her text as a third reviewer looking for problems that she *could* address – unlike the commercial confidentiality problem, which she could not. What seemed to be missing, from my outsider perspective, was a confident statement of the paper's purpose and an argument about its significance in relation to previous work in her field.

As her publication broker, I initiated discussion about these issues, asking Rajee to talk further about the significance of her work in her field. A useful move was to ask her to do a writing exercise from Kamler and Thomson (2006) called syntactic borrowing. In this exercise, a passage from an already published article is selected and the content is deleted, so that what remains is the sentence skeleton (Swales and Feak, 1994). Less experienced writers like Rajee are asked to insert the details of their own research into the skeleton structure:

> The skeleton creates a linguistic frame to play with. It encourages writers to take on the subject position of an experienced, authoritative writer . . . they may not be able to take by themselves.
>
> (Kamler and Thomson, 2006: 57)

Figure 5.1 shows Rajee's use of a skeleton passage by Lavie (2006) from the *Education Administration Quarterly*, a journal outside her field. The italicized text designates the language used by Lavie.

> *In this article, I discuss the main arguments that deal with* the optimisation of Finite Element Models (FEM). *In distinguishing between* optimized and non-optimized structures, *it is my purpose to highlight* the advantages of an optimized structure *by pointing to* weight and cost reductions. *Besides providing a map of the* methodologies used, *I assess the extent to which* these techniques lay groundwork to improve the structure.
>
> *The article is structured as follows. After giving an overview of the scope* of 'shape optimization', *I review* the mathematical background of the optimization process. *Next I provide a summary of* the ReSHAPE software, including the processes that can be employed in the optimization process. *Finally, in the last two sections, I consider* the approach to analysis and results derived from the FEM which is optimized with ReSHAPE *and argue that* the optimized structure is lighter and more efficient than the non-optimized structure.

Figure 5.1 Rajee's syntactic borrowing using Lavie (2006).

This exercise had powerful effects for Rajee. It helped her articulate the purpose of her research and take on a more authoritative discursive stance clearly missing in her initial submission. By borrowing Lavie's syntax, she found authoritative language she could use to situate her own research. She did not simply insert this exercise into her revised article, but it helped her learn how to argue for the distinctiveness of her contribution. It provided a scaffold for experimenting with new ways of representing herself as a more assured scholar in the field of aeronautical engineering.

In an email communication with Rajee, she later said the exercise 'made all the difference' to imagining how to distinguish 'my research without compromising confidentiality agreements'. In her final published article I was pleased to see traces of a new textual confidence about the value of her work: 'Shape optimisation enables weight savings as well as long term cost benefits, while ensuring the component is structurally sound and can be commercially manufactured.' Her aeronautical engineering colleagues had not greatly assisted her in this work; the editor had simply asked her to attend to the reviewer comments and the reviewers had given her little material to work with. Without a broker mediating reviewer reports and exploring possible directions for revision, it was all guesswork.

A somewhat different situation arose for Sam, who was more devastated than confused by the reviewer reports she received, and brought these to me, in my role as her doctoral supervisor. My aim was to move Sam beyond her distress and decision to 'bin' the article. The key pedagogic move was to conduct a joint analysis of the reviewer reports. I stressed that the two reviewers had differences of opinion and that it was not warranted to assume the more negative commentary was more correct. We looked at how the reviewers differed and where their differences cancelled each other out. We also looked at where reviewers agreed. Both had rated the significance of the paper and its appropriateness for the journal as medium – perhaps not as desirable as high, but certainly not low.

I then did a closer analysis of the more negative report, which Sam read as damning evidence of her scholarly incompetence. In this excerpt from the reviewer report, Sam's methodological work is severely criticized, particularly her failure to acknowledge significant previous research on patterns of classroom discourse:

> There is a very unfortunate misunderstanding of the way in which IRE formats work in classrooms. This might stem from the fact that much of the foundational work in the area is not cited in this paper – eg Baker; McHoul; Cazden; Mehan etc and more recently researchers such as Groves, Comber, Lin and the work out of NIE in Singapore. The IRE format works as it does because it places the teacher in charge of turn taking and basically turns multiparty talk into two party talk . . . You'll note that the sequence that the 'new' structure proposes in this paper does not vary from traditional IRE formats in this regard at all. I would consequently question if this new format is indeed in any way innovative or new on the dimensions that the paper claims. I find this to be a major flaw in the research reported within the paper and I believe that the author should take account of the extensive work which has been conducted around lesson structures and IRE within classrooms in order to review the claims made within the paper.

The critique is stated in harsh terms and makes assumptions about what Sam does not know. Her failure to situate her work in relation to an already established literature leads the reviewer to question whether the pattern of teacher discourse she proposes is new or innovative in any way. The imperious tone and assumption that Sam did not know the literature is unnecessarily condescending. But from my perspective the feedback was useful, as it highlighted a serious omission Sam needed to address if her claim to innovation was going to stand up.

Sam actually knew this literature quite well, but had not used it sufficiently to make her case. When we looked more closely at her submitted article, we found she had devoted only one cursory paragraph to the IRE literature and made no link to her own work. Subsequently, she re-immersed herself in this literature and redrafted the article a number of times to engage with the critique and reconceptualize her analysis in more comparative terms. Recontextualizing her research in this way – for a wider audience and in relation to previous scholarship – is an absolutely crucial task for any doctoral writer seeking publication outside the dissertation. (For a more detailed account see Lee and Kamler, 2008.)

If we think about Rajee and Sam's experiences in discursive terms, it is clear that both writers needed brokering to engage satisfactorily with the reviewer commentary. Mediation was needed to read between the lines of disciplinary conversations (about commercial confidentiality or previous classroom discourse research) and then to provide concrete suggestions and modes of action to make the revision possible. Pedagogically, the broker modelled a critical reading strategy that neither could accomplish on her own, but which foregrounded the discursive nature of the evaluations received. Such intervention diffused the emotionality (Sam) and confusion (Rajee) that early career writers often experience. It also repositioned them as strategic academics who can engage with critique and take action. Such action led to successful publication for both writers.

It is worth pointing out that editors can also play a significant brokering role in guiding writers about how to negotiate reviewer critique (Wellington, 2003). Neither Sam nor Rajee received this kind of support and both were simply told to attend to the comments from reviewers. This seemingly neutral stance does not consider any of the discursive complexities I have tried to tease out. The editors I interviewed while writing this chapter, by contrast, were more self-conscious about the partial and sometimes contradictory nature of the reviewer reports they receive and the need to mediate these. One editor wrote:

> So, in some cases it seems to me that our job as editors is to help articulate the confusion, under writing, under reporting, or inadequacy of the study indexed by the reviewers' comments. But, in other cases it seems to me our task is to articulate the differing epistemological and ontological positions of the reviewers . . . Thus, it does not seem appropriate for an editor to merely pass the reviewers' comments on to the author without framing them and incorporating them into a coherent response from the editors.
>
> (Personal communication with editor)

Clearly, less experienced writers would benefit from such editorial mediation, as would the brokers who guide novice writer resubmissions. This editor's commentary, however, also raises issues about how explicitly pedagogic a role editors should play in the peer review process, a matter to which I return at the conclusion of the chapter.

Writing letters to the editor

Having been guided by a publication broker to negotiate reviewers' concerns, a final task for the writer is to communicate these decisions to the editor. The editor is the final arbiter of the review process. She both commissions and mediates the reviewer reports and uses these to make final judgements about the article's relevance and potential contribution. What stance do novice researchers take when telling a more experienced and powerful editor how they have attended to the reviewer advice and/or where they may have not?

In revise and resubmit letters, editors always ask writers for a clear documentation of the changes made. Writers may respond in a variety of ways to this request. Here I look at three different approaches. I return to Sam, as a case of an inexperienced doctoral writer learning how to respond to editors. I then consider two cases of more experienced co-authors: Andrea and Carolyn dealing with fairly straightforward critique; and Beatrice and Tina negotiating a lengthy and difficult set of reviewer demands over a protracted period of time. My purpose in looking at a continuum of response is to tease out questions of power and authority. I am interested in how the discursive stance taken by writers is shaped by their experience, confidence and status in the field. I want to counter the notion, again, that there is simply a set procedure or a formulaic genre for writers to follow in communicating with editors.

Sam writes back to the editor

The editor who communicated with Sam suggested that, when she attended to reviewer comments, she should use track changes to communicate where revisions had been made. As her supervisor, I suggested a different procedure. Track changes in this instance seemed to position Sam as a novice follower of expert advice. My goal, by contrast, was to position her with greater agency. So I suggested she create a chart to document the changes she made, a strategy used by many experienced writers. Table 5.1 shows an excerpt from the chart Sam sent back to the editor.

Table 5.1 Excerpt from chart of changes to resubmitted article

Reviewer's comments	Changes/revisions
Key concern of Reviewer 2 Possible misrepresentation of IRE/IRF pattern and the reasons it constructs students differentially	pp. 5–6, paras 1, 2, 3, 4 and 5 Fuller and more balanced (i.e. not so negative) discussion of aspects and debate about the IRF pattern, acknowledging similarities between IRF and proposed pattern
Proposed new pattern does not vary in these ways and would question whether the new format is innovative in the way the paper claims	p. 5, para. 4 More refined focus on the fact that it is the centrality of questions as the initiating move in IRF that the new pattern rewrites, and more provisional approach to researching effects of this change

Source: Lee and Kamler (2008: 521).

We might characterize the discursive stance taken in Sam's two-column graphic representation as compliant yet confident. On the left she summarizes the key reviewer commentary she is addressing; on the right she documents what she has changed and its location in her text (by page and paragraph number). There is no disagreeing with reviewers. She takes on their key criticisms and responds. Guidance from her broker/supervisor made it clear that the advice was valuable for the article and her thesis. Her representation in the chart shows her engaging the review process as a dialogic exchange, rather than as a set of commands. She does not list every reviewer query she received, but shows the serious way she has revised using their advice, for the better.

The extended publication exchange with her supervisor as broker brought Sam inside a set of publishing practices previously unknown to her. She learned about the partiality and textual nature of reviewer commentary and moved beyond the pain of critique. She took reviewer advice and used it, but selectively and in relation to furthering her own purposes in the article and the dissertation itself.

Carolyn and Andrea debate the reviewers

The second example comes from two experienced writers who co-authored a text for a higher education journal. Carolyn and Andrea (pseudonyms) received two reviewer reports, one mostly positive, the other with a number of issues to address. Their letter begins by addressing the editor: 'Thank you very much for your email of 20 July notifying us of the referees' responses to our submitted article. We have revised our paper in response to the referees' comments as follows.' They then directly address the two referees in turn.

In Table 5.2, I set out the more critical referee report in the left column, and the author response in the right. Carolyn and Andrea did not use this chart format in communicating with the editor, but I have adopted it here to highlight the way they seem to mimic the pithy style of the referee's six bullet points. They respond with five terse and somewhat combative points.

We might characterize this exchange between referee and authors as a debate. Referee 1 is not satisfied with the information offered and wants more concrete examples. In point 1 she wants more on policy agendas; in points 2 and 4, more on the case studies; in 3, more on disciplines that do not accept a post-positivist paradigm. Points 5 and 6 ask for improved editing.

Carolyn and Andrea clearly do not take up the compliant stance demonstrated by Sam. They have points they wish to argue with the reviewer and highlight these in a business-like manner. Using the extended metaphor of the debate we might characterize their moves as follows. In point 1, they debate and concede. They clarify that their focus is not on policy, but they concede by making token reference to recent policy agendas. In point 2,

Table 5.2 Authors respond to Referee I report

Referee I report	Author response
• The paper refers to a policy agenda that creates writing problems and then responds to them – if in a less than effective manner. It would be helpful if the paper could make more reference to concrete examples of this policy agenda (e.g. QAA in UK) which is looking closely at research supervision.	While it was not our intention to engage in the policy process per se, we have made brief reference to the QAA in the UK and the RTS in Australia where relevant.
• The paper refers to the disciplinary contexts within which research writing takes place but the two case studies give little insight into how such contexts might play a part in the work RWGs do. Please give more details and examples.	We acknowledge the request for detail of disciplinary contexts for RWGs. We want to stress that specific disciplinary work has not been the purpose of these particular groups. We do agree there is a need for more studies of the kind suggested here.
• The paper assumes a post-positivist/ realist context within which writing problems are situated. What about disciplines that do not recognize such a context and/or disciplines that continue to conduct research in a positivistic/ realist fashion? Please say more about this.	We have amended the article to suggest that these writing group pedagogies have been used within science-based disciplines and in interdisciplinary contexts, as is the case with case study I.
• Some reference to participant voices in the case study accounts would be helpful.	We respond by saying that student voices do appear in earlier work cited as the basis for the case studies (Saunders, Sampson and Lee 1999, Aitchison 2000, Lee and Boud 2003). This article seeks to theorize from these earlier accounts to build a basis for curriculum development. We are currently involved in preparing a further article with participants who are research degree candidates at UTS and members of a doctoral writing group.
• I thought the paper was too long. It could be tightened and still communicate the main points.	We acknowledge points 5 and 6 and have tightened the argument accordingly and edited the text.
• Please proofread again. There are a number of typos in the paper I received.	

they debate and partially concede. They argue that their purpose in the case studies was not disciplinary work, but concede the reviewer's point, *beyond* the article: yes, there need to be more case studies of this kind, but not by them and not here. In point 3, they concede. They clarify that writing groups do operate in broader disciplines and add this information. In point 4 they acknowledge the referee's request for student voices, but refuse by clarifying where, when and how they have incorporated voice in their previous work. The implication is that the referee has misunderstood the more theoretical intent of this article. In points 5 and 6 the authors simply concede to the less controversial request to tighten and proofread their writing.

Their second referee report set out its concerns in a more collegial manner and certainly not as a list of errors to be corrected. First it outlined the strengths of the article: the significance of its topic, the expert knowledge of the writers, the soundness of their argument; then it made one major criticism:

> There is only one issue that I would like to challenge the authors to consider: in their depiction of the formation of research writing groups, the impression one gets is that such groups are free from conflict and tensions, and as a result, while the proposals are most commendable, they appear to me to lack credibility unless the very real difficulties such groups are bound to encounter are both acknowledged and 'theorized'. Other than that, I strongly recommend that this paper be accepted for publication.
>
> (Excerpt from Referee 2 report)

It is this point that Andrea and Carolyn address in their response, but they do so in two sentences only:

> This report challenges us to consider the question of conflict and tension. We acknowledge this point in the concluding section of the article, but agree that these matters will need to be further theorized in order to build a credible and sustainable curriculum development for research writing.

Even in this brief reply Andrea and Carolyn appear to make three moves. The first is to acknowledge the force of the reviewer's concern (*challenges us to consider the question of conflict and tension*) and agree she's made an important point. The second is to partially agree with the reviewer and indicate where in the revised article her concern has been addressed (*We acknowledge this point in the concluding section of the article*). The third move offers a rebuttal. They agree about the need for further theorizing, but not in this article. Their tactic, however, is less combative, possibly in response to this referee's more generous stance: they include the reviewer in the collective work the field needs to do in order to build a credible research writing curriculum.

Taken together, the positional work Andrea and Carolyn achieve in their two replies to referees is complex yet succinct. They are not defensive, but strongly defend the purpose of their article and refute commentary that will take them in a different direction. It is in part because Referee 2 is so positive and seems to 'get' what they do that they are able to refute many of Referee 1's points. They articulate reasons why they will not take up all the advice offered, but seem confident that their rebuttals will be accepted by the editor.

It is neither possible nor appropriate to imagine inexperienced writers like Sam taking a similar discursive stance. Carolyn and Andrea are positioned differently in the academy and have the confidence to adopt this more assertive approach. That said, Andrea took the lead in framing these responses, as Carolyn had not yet published extensively and was simultaneously preparing publications from her own PhD. Carolyn described her initial reaction to their stance as 'scary', but appreciated the way co-authorship brokered her understanding of ways to interact with more powerful players in the publication game and still hold to the integrity of their work.

Beatrice and Tina argue with the editor

The final example of writing to editors comes from two experienced academics who co-authored a text for a high-status education research journal. If Carolyn and Andrea's interactions were brief and unproblematic, the opposite was the case for Tina and Beatrice (pseudonyms), who negotiated four revisions and five complicated communications with the editor.

Beatrice and Tina's first review was an 11-page critique from three referees, the editor and a student advisory board. The commentary was structured under under eight headings: (1) Contribution to the Literature; (2) Conceptual/Theoretical Framework; (3) Supporting Evidence; (4) Clarity, Coherence, Focus, and Accuracy; (5) Grammatical and Typographical Errors; (6) APA Errors; (7) Reference List Errors; (8) Citation Errors. Points 1–5 were a synthesis of reviewers' key points whereas points 6–8 came directly from the editor. The editor also attached the three referee reports with a strongly stated encouragement to persevere: 'Thus, our encouragement for you to revise your manuscript is an extremely strong one.'

Despite this encouragement, the sheer weight of the commentary created a negative tone. In places the address to authors was insulting: 'Throughout the manuscript, there are violations to American Psychological Association (APA) guidelines'; and reviewer requests for empirical data seemed entirely at odds with the authors' use of textual analysis in the article as a form of inquiry. Tina wanted to withdraw the manuscript, but Beatrice was keen to persevere so she took the lead in better foregrounding their theoretical framework and making their text analytic work more explicit. Multiple drafts of the revision and a five-page response to the editor were crafted to clarify how they had addressed the reviewers' concerns.

The second letter from the editor, arriving two months later, commended Beatrice and Tina on their revised manuscript, but comprised 13 pages of multiple requests and dissatisfactions, set out under the same headings as the first letter. Beatrice and Tina were shocked to find the manuscript had not

Table 5.3 Authors respond to editor after second revision

Comment	Response
(1) New reviewers have been added.	This produces new requirements which may not satisfy the original referees. There is a danger of setting up a circuitous process of change. We have therefore decided to prioritize the recommendations of our original referees as we understand them to have been represented (D, E, G). We note that Reviewer D says that the article is ready for publication.
(2) Reviewers have mixed recommendations.	This is inevitable. Part of the editorial process as we understand it is to indicate which referees' comments can be ignored and which ought to be dealt with. We have made the decision to follow the original referees, which is how we interpret the editor's comments, and take up as much of the new commentary as we can within the word limitations.
(5) Reviewer E requests more explicit information about how the texts we recommend differ from those that we critique.	Reviewer E suggests a useful set of phrases for inclusion. We have largely paraphrased these at the end of the section. Reviewer F also asked for more details of recommended texts. This might satisfy F although, given that she/he felt the article should be rejected, we can only assume that she/he requires a full book review rather than an argued opinion.
(6) Reviewer E is concerned about our use of 'dangling' rhetorical questions on p. 8. She/he suggests that at a minimum readers need to have citations that can be followed up.	We have added citations in an endnote (3) about work intensification and performative regimes of universities.
(9) Reviewer A wants a more detailed analytic framing which shows more of the actual workings of the analysis.	This would take up more space than is possible. We have inserted a little more detail about the process of content analysis. We note that Reviewer B praises the 'sophisticated' framing.
(11) Reviewer A seems to think we are endorsing the notion that experience is a sufficient basis on which to write advice. She/he then suggests that this is problematic. That it is problematic is precisely the point we are making and we think this is clear in the text.	We have not amended the point since we think it is clear. Certainly Reviewers C, D, E and G get the point.

Comment	Response
(14) Reviewer B argues that the lack of examples may cause harm to some writers of advice books.	We agree that there is a conflict between evidence and ethics, but our experience suggests that it is exactly the reverse of Reviewer B's suggestion (which is of course an opinion). We have now inserted a footnote (2) to explain the potential evidence versus ethics issue as we know it.
(17) One of the grammatical errors needing change – is p. 10 their authority should be plural.	The suggested change is ungrammatical. Our text is correct.

only been sent back to previous reviewers, but sent to four new ones as well. The overall judgement was: four for acceptance with minor changes; one for full revise/resubmit; two for rejection. Nevertheless, the editor intensified his encouragement for them to further revise the manuscript.

At this point Beatrice was ready to give up. She believed that, although the initial reviewers were mostly satisfied, the new reviewers had compiled an array of analytic and interpretive issues too extensive to address. She could not tolerate the prospect of endless cycles of revision, as one set of reviewers was pleased, only to be contradicted by the next. This time Tina, who felt too invested in the article to let it go, took the lead in round two revisions. Table 5.3 sets out a brief excerpt from their lengthy response to the editor, originally represented as a chart of 19 items.

The discursive stance taken here, like that of Carolyn and Andrea's, is one of debate, but in this case it has become protracted and combative. Sometimes substantive points are argued, sometimes the reviewers themselves are critiqued and sometimes the journal practices are put under scrutiny, such as sending the revised article out to a new set of reviewers. Tina and Beatrice are explicit about how they have interpreted and prioritized the reviews: where they have agreed with reviewers and inserted text (5, 6, 14); where they have disagreed and/or ignored the reviewer commentary (11, 17); where they have partially conceded (9) using other reviewer opinion as support.

It is worth noting that the editor did not simply accept their rebuttal, but responded as an equally assertive and robust participant in the debate, ultimately with greater power. In his third letter he argued:

The rationales given by the authors for not addressing some of these comments included the following: 'This would take up more space than is possible' . . . 'It would not be possible to do anything other than an unsatisfactory passing comment within this word limit.' We would like to bring to the attention of the authors the fact that the word limits only pertain to the initial submission. Thus, it is essential that the authors do not use concerns about word limits to prevent them from fully addressing the reviewers' comments.

The process did not end here. Subsequent to the acceptance of their article for publication, there were two further revisions handled internally by the editor and his student advisory board. Although Tina and Beatrice had no external broker to sustain them through the process, their co-authorship clearly played a critical role in maintaining their stamina. They seemed to adopt this brokering role alternately. As one flagged the other took up the baton and led the running; then the other jumped in to participate again in the revising. The need for mutual support continued right to the end as further demands were made through three sets of track changes for revision of syntax, 'colloquialisms' and 'APA violations'.

Beatrice and Tina's annoyance escalated over time as they failed to counter what they saw as unreasonable demands to homogenize their writing style. When in the last stages the editor gave them tight deadlines because the article was already scheduled for publication, Tina and Beatrice began to understand that they did have some power in the situation. The editor recognized their position in his penultimate communication when he wrote: 'While we recognize that you will likely disagree with the few remaining phrases we have asked you to reword, we hope you will agree to do so.' In the end they did agree in order to get published, perhaps giving some credence to Frey's (2003: 205) extreme claim that the only way to get papers published is to 'intellectually prostitute oneself'.

Whereas Tina and Beatrice saw themselves as previously skilful in negotiating reviewer demands, here they felt both demoralized and angry. Their discursive stance is not recommended for novices but must be contextualized in five months of constant editorial demands balanced by escalating editor assurances that the journal *really* wanted their article (e.g. 'Thus, our encouragement for you to revise your manuscript is even stronger than previously'). Without this encouragement and their mutual brokering they would not have succeeded in finally seeing their article in print.

Conclusion

In this chapter I have argued for publication brokering that supports early career writers in publishing their research. I have explored this brokering as a social discursive practice to make explicit the complex social, cultural and political dimensions of revise and resubmit that require mediation. In theorizing this pedagogy I am working against formulaic, how-to approaches that represent the process of responding to reviewers and editors as straightforward and unproblematic.

The stories I have told in this chapter demonstrate the opposite. Rajee and Sam as the least experienced academics clearly needed a broker to interpret and strategize – to guide their reading of reviewer reports and figure out what was required to make an effective revision. Neither received help from editors and reviewer commentary did not provide sufficient guidance for Rajee.

But the more experienced and previously published writers in this chapter also needed brokering assistance. Carolyn and Andrea and Beatrice and Tina brokered each other in negotiating difficult reviewer and/or editor demands they were not willing to accept. Their letters to their editors demonstrate that writers need not slavishly follow the demands made by anonymous referees. Whereas their discursive stance of debate and contest will not be appropriate for researchers in the earliest stages of their career, it is important for brokers to help all writers gain agency in the revise and resubmit process.

Recently Staller (2007) has argued that crucial discussions occur during the review process that shape scholarship; that authors, editors and referees often 'joust' during review and such practices should be made public – rather than shrouded in the accepted norms of silence and privacy that characterize the peer review process. My explorations of a revise and resubmit pedagogy are offered in this spirit and to raise awareness about the critical role of the publication broker in this work.

Given the increasing pressures on doctoral researchers to publish during and after candidature, the need for brokering will only increase. But who should do the brokering? In this chapter I have illustrated brokering work from the position of external consultant, doctoral supervisor and academic colleague. In other chapters of this volume, we see the potential of writing groups and senior academic colleagues as publication brokers. I would argue that there is also an essential role to be played by journal editors. My interviews with editors and those reported by Wellington (2003) suggest that many editors recognize the complex, sometimes methodologically hostile and contradictory advice offered in reviewer reports and the need to guide authors about how to negotiate these. They take an active role in synthesizing and giving direction – which advice to attend to fully, which to background, perhaps which to ignore.

Neutral form letters that ask writers to simply attend to reviewer advice and return their manuscript showing revisions through track changes seriously minimize and misrepresent the process. Revise and resubmit entails complex discursive, social and emotional work that needs expert mediation from a variety of academic players, editors included. There is too much to learn and too much at stake for early career writers to do this work alone.

References

Casanave, C. P. and Vandrick, S. (eds) (2003) *Writing for Scholarly Publication: Behind the Scenes in Language Education*, Mahwah, NJ: Lawrence Erlbaum.

Frey, B. (2003) 'Publishing as Prostitution?: Choosing between One's Own Ideas and Academic Success', *Public Choice*, 116 (1–2), 205–23.

Hartley, J. (2008) *Academic Writing and Publishing: A Practical Handbook*, London: Routledge.

Kamler, B. and Thomson, P. (2006) *Helping Doctoral Students Write: Pedagogies for Supervision*. London: Routledge.

Kamler, B. and Thomson, P. (2008) 'The Failure of Dissertation Advice Books: Towards Alternative Pedagogies for Doctoral Writing', *Educational Researcher*, 37 (8), 507–18.

Kubota, R. (2003) 'Striving for Original Voice in Publication?: A Critical Reflection', in C. P. Casanave and S. Vandrick (eds) *Writing for Scholarly Publication: Behind the Scenes in Language Education*, Mahwah, NJ: Lawrence Erlbaum Associates, pp. 61–72.

Lavie, J. (2006) 'Academic Discourses on School-Based Teacher Collaboration: Revisiting the Arguments', *Education Administration Quarterly*, 42 (5), 773–805.

Lee, A. and Kamler, B. (2008) 'Bringing Pedagogy to Doctoral Publishing', *Teaching in Higher Education*, 13 (5), 511–23.

Lillis T. and Curry, M. (2006) 'Professional Academic Writing by Multilingual Scholars: Interactions with Literacy Brokers in the Production of English-Medium Texts', *Written Communication*, 23 (1), 3–35.

Murray, R. (2005) *Writing for Academic Journals*, Buckingham: Open University Press.

Staller, K. (2007) 'Metalogue as Methodology: Inquiries into Conversations among Authors, Editors and Referees', *Qualitative Social Work*, 6 (2), 137–57.

Swales, J. M. and Feak, C. B. (1994) *Academic Writing for Graduate Students: Essential Tasks and Skills,* Ann Arbor, MI: University of Michigan Press.

Thomson, P. and Kamler, B. (2009, in press) 'It's Been Said Before and We'll Say It Again: Research *Is* Writing', in P. Thomson and M. Walker (eds) *The Doctoral Companion Handbook*, London: Routledge.

Wellington, J. (2003) *Getting Published: A Guide for Lecturers and Researchers*, London: Routledge Falmer.

Chapter 6

Learning together to publish

Writing group pedagogies for doctoral publishing

Claire Aitchison

Introduction

Writing groups have long been a part of the educational landscape. In some contexts writing groups are formal, perhaps even assessable, components of a course of study; elsewhere they are ad hoc, external or adjunct to institutionally prescribed teaching and learning (Gere, 1987). This chapter examines a relatively new phenomenon – writing groups for doctoral students that support their writing of the thesis and writing for publication.

Recent accounts of writing groups in higher education attend to institutional and policy agendas for improved writing and writing output (Cuthbert and Spark, 2008; McGrail, Rickard and Jones, 2006; Murray, 2005). Much current literature reports on participant satisfaction and productivity (Galligan, Cretchley, George, Martin-McDonald and McDonald, 2003; Larcombe, McCosker and O'Loughlin, 2007; Page-Adams and Cheng, 1994). What I want to do here is to build on these perspectives by attending to less-often-told accounts of the pedagogical practices of writing groups in order to capture something of the real life of writing groups that is frequently flattened out in analysis. I do this by infusing my account with the voices of participants from my own facilitation of, and research into, writing groups (Aitchison, 2003, 2009) and through semi-fictionalized illustrative stories drawn from practice and theorizing (Aitchison and Lee, 2006; Lee and Aitchison, 2009). I take this approach because writing group practices remain under-studied – and yet when I am asked to speak about doctoral writing groups I am *always* asked about the everyday nitty-gritty of how they work; how students actually learn together and how facilitators can make groups work successfully.

My knowledge of writing group pedagogies has been informed by my work as an academic literacies lecturer responsible for a university-wide programme of writing groups for higher degree research students. Eight years ago, these groups had an explicit focus on writing the thesis; however, over time, participants have brought an expanding repertoire of research writing to these groups. This development has arisen in part from

changing university requirements for more compulsory written documentation, including confirmation of candidature documents, ethics applications
and university conference papers. Equally however, we have witnessed an
increase in student-driven desire to write for publication in the scholarly and
popular press.

In response, our writing groups have altered and evolved, and we have
trialled a variety of pedagogical models. Broadly speaking there are now two
kinds of groups: a 21-hour weekly programme focusing on thesis writing
with a negotiated curriculum taught over nine weeks; and a programme of
ongoing writing groups that meet fortnightly, where students share a wide
variety of research texts. To date we have offered 11 course-length writing
group programmes and have had up to six ongoing groups at any one time.
Groups tend to have a core membership of six to eight people with a functional upper limit of 12. All groups are interdisciplinary and participation is
voluntary.

This chapter is arranged around a semi-fictionalized story of one writing group meeting. The story is told in two parts mirroring my two central
concerns and the structure of this chapter: first, how doctoral students learn
key practices for writing for publication as they work together in writing
groups; and, second, the role of the facilitator in this endeavour.

Student peer review as pedagogy

Scenario one – Writing group tales: 'new girl' learns the ropes

Individuals arrive within minutes of each other. Today a new person is joining
us; another we haven't seen for months because she's been teaching intensively
to supplement the family income before her final semester of doctoral candidature. There is talk about old members, forthcoming conferences, supervisors,
the comings and goings of people's lives.

These conversations are broken into by me, directing the group's attention
to our busy programme. The noise settles. I begin by introducing the new
person and initiating round-the-room introductions. Devi introduces herself
and her research by talking us through her Table of Contents. Although the
others have heard it before, I briefly outline how our group operates; about
circulating writing, keeping confidences and giving and receiving feedback. As
I give Devi some handouts reiterating these matters, I notice one of today's
text volunteers is getting anxious. I know she is worried that our reviewing
time is dwindling, so I hurriedly check the schedule of writing for the next few
meetings. Then we get on to the real agenda.

The first text volunteer, Marianne, reminds us about her struggles with this draft and the kind of feedback she'd like. That familiar moment again – the pause before anyone responds to my prompt 'Who would like to start off with some feedback for Marianne?' I wait and then listen as the pace, colour and tempo change from the first tentative comments through the rise and fall of agreement and disagreement, clarifications, the occasional oppositional opinion, the laughter, the enjoyment, the struggle. This group is fabulous. Most of the current members have been together for 14 months and most are in mid-to-late candidature, having seen others complete their dissertations over recent months.

As the hour closes I have little extra to add: my key points reiterate and summarize much of what has already been discussed as I seek to clarify the future direction Marianne may take in revising her text. Most of us seem to think the metadiscourse is overdone; we have worried about the over-reliance on tables and advocate a return to a narrative style more in keeping with the methodological approach; we suggest more thinking about the structure. We recognize the text as early-stage thinking and therefore early-stage writing. It's a bit clunky. The challenge is how to write oneself into the project, to know what is at issue here from the data and how the story should be told. People return to Marianne their written-upon copies of her chapter.

It's break time and the call for 'Coffee' – and today it's cherry cake.

I begin with this semi-fictionalized retelling of my most recent writing group meeting because this anecdotal account shows the twin concerns that are typically played out around writing: the interplay between meaning and its articulation. It is this very difficult and shifting territory that energizes group interactions, and it is precisely what is at issue for doctoral students struggling to 'know' and to express that knowledge as particular kinds of disciplinary scholars for particular kinds of readers.

For doctoral students, gaining the necessary knowledge of their discipline, topic and research can take considerable time and effort. In this anecdote Marianne admits she's been having trouble with her draft and it's obvious that she regards the process of feedback and discussion from her peers as a vital part of her practice for developing her writing. Writing plays an important role in students' 'coming to know' (Jones, Turner and Street, 1999; Lillis, 2001; Richardson, 2000), as it is through the writing, and discussion of that writing, that scholarly knowledge and identity are explored and tested out. In this sense, writing groups exemplify a pedagogy that realizes writing as social practice because, in writing groups, writing is both produced through social interaction and is the outcome of social interaction. Writing group participants write together informed by other social networks such as disciplinary scholars, supervisors and institutional stakeholders. In writing groups for doctoral students, this 'becoming scholar' can develop a familiarity with the conversations and discoursal practices of their disciplinary community as they learn to communicate effectively. Writing groups provide students with multiple opportunities to develop both the knowledge and writing know-how for publishing their work.

Excerpts from transcripts of actual writing group discussions illustrate how the interplay between coming to know and meaning-making plays out around writing.

Writing to know and knowing how to write

The most common request made by peers in writing groups is 'Does it make sense?' This concern speaks to the desire of both readers and authors to have writing communicate meaningfully. In writing groups we witness 'the history of writers' intentions around meaning making' (Lillis, 2001: 27) because private thinking becomes public as it is written, shared and discussed. To illustrate how this process works in the context of doctoral writing groups, I discuss two excerpts from a transcript of a group meeting in which the author and reviewing peers interpret, interrogate, rework and clarify meaning – and attend to its written articulation.

This writing group had been meeting fortnightly for six months. Half of the group aimed to complete their PhD within 12 months. Two students came from the natural sciences, but otherwise the social sciences predominated, as did qualitative and mixed methods research approaches.

The text under discussion is an early draft which had been circulated by email to members a week prior to the meeting and comprised five pages of a methodological section that the writer, Matthew, had been struggling with. Not surprisingly, much of the discussion centred around the meaning of key concepts. Participants sought additional explanation and clarification, by asking, for example: 'What do you mean here?', 'Is that meant to imply . . . ?', 'It's just that when I read that, not knowing the background, I thought . . .', and 'I just wasn't sure what you were talking about . . .' Gere (1987) argues that interactions of this kind foster learning:

> Participants in collaborative groups learn when they challenge one another with questions, when they use the evidence and information available to them, when they develop relationships among issues, when they evaluate their own thinking. In other words, they learn when they assume that knowledge is something they can help create rather than something to be received whole from someone else.
>
> (Gere, 1987:69)

I argue that peer interaction in writing groups is doubly powerful because peers test and extend their conceptual knowledge as well as their capacity to communicate this knowledge through writing. In this example, after an extended exchange about the theoretical and conceptual dimensions of constructivism, Matthew moves the attention of the group from the concepts, to how he has written about them. The transcript excerpt below exemplifies the way meaning-making talk can generate discussion about how to express meaning.

Excerpt One – Writing group transcript

Matthew:	By the way though, may I ask: is this understandable?
Claire:	Oh yeah.
Jane:	Yeah, it's really good.
Matthew:	It's logical. It's not logical as much as I'd like, but . . .
Louise:	But just to pick up, I mean, I kind of can't really connect with what you're saying, and it all seems just a bit thin there, and I think that you need to flesh that out a little bit – or say that you are going to flesh that out somewhere else.
Matthew:	Yeah, yeah.
Mary:	Maybe like a line that connects you into that next section on the neoliberal institutionalism that we were just talking about?
Louise:	Yeah, just something, because you point forward as if you're going to talk about it later on.

Here Matthew and his peers are trying to understand both the theory and concepts at issue in this piece of writing *and* the articulation of this knowledge. As evidenced in this transcript excerpt: coming to know *and* the articulation of that knowledge are intimately entwined.

This ability to articulate what is known through written language is especially pertinent for scholars wishing to publish their work, since they must be able not only to show their expert knowledge, but to express it according to the expectations of particular networks of scholarly publishers and readers. This meaning-making is rhetorical and political and requires more than simple clarity of understanding and expression. It requires that writers be able to position themselves within their particular discourse community, and this depends on the writer being aware of the community's interests, debates, norms and expectations.

In the next part of this same writing group discussion, members question and probe Matthew, helping him pinpoint exactly the concerns of his discipline.

Excerpt Two – Writing group transcript

Mary:	. . . just on the topic of headings, when you said 'Privileging of agency over structure' on page 4, the word 'privilege' has a lot of meaning in terms of power knowledge so I'm wondering if that's something that you want to try and flesh out a little more or try and play with or whatever.
Matthew:	Well you notice I'm starting to play with it here, I quite agree with you, because I'll make it a bigger, stronger argument, and that one of the major contentions within the field is this power agency thing.
Claire:	So maybe you could have that as a heading: Contested territory, agency and structure?
Matthew:	Nah, 'Contested meanings'.
Claire:	Yeah, that could be.
Louise:	Yeah.
Claire:	Something like that.
Mary:	Just to sort of show that there is a problematic there. Because it sort of, at the moment its unproblematic. It's sort of written like . . . there's no issue.
Karen:	Where is the issue?
Matthew:	Yeah. OK, so I'll start it Contested meanings, does social construction privilege agency over structure?
Claire:	Yes, something like that.
Matthew:	Yes.
Louise:	That provides the intellectual contestation. That's what it's all about, isn't it?
Catherine:	Well, I think that there is another title that's needed, before you get to the end. And that is the notion of policy. So that you go from saying that there is this problematic, this contestation, but now you are going to lead us to the point that you're pinpointing your investigation of where that contest happens. And that's in policy. And because that sets up what you are going to investigate for the rest of your thesis. That lets someone say 'oh well, let's go to the statistics, we'll look at the statistics, and that'll show something', or 'let's go to, I don't know, media reviews.' But you're going to policy, and I think that's a really important thing that you do differently to anyone else that is looking at the issue.
Claire:	In a sense it's kind of a gap isn't it? Fill the gap. Are we right Matthew or what do you think?
Catherine:	No one else has done that, have they Matthew?
Matthew:	Oh I'm not sure yet, I have to think about that one.

In response to a query about his use of headings, Matthew acknowledges that he needs to work further on one of the key debates within his discipline: 'this power agency thing'. He accepts Mary's proposal that he attend to the problematic and the group offers suggestions for a new reworded heading. Importantly, the group's concern is no longer simply that his meaning be clear. They share now an additional objective, which is to position the writing within a wider debate to 'show that there is a problematic'.

Integral to the talk about how the author wishes to position himself in regard to the concerns of his field is a close attention to the actual wording of the heading itself. After discussing, rejecting and modifying suggestions, Matthew arrives at a new heading, about which Louise declares: 'That provides the intellectual contestation. That's what it's all about, isn't it?'. The group has resolved a reworking of text that both provides clarity *and* resituates the author's argument within existing debates. But the rhetorical work is not yet concluded; Catherine suggests that Matthew explicitly move his argument further on by creating 'another title'.

Catherine is aware of the importance of making a new contribution to knowledge within academic scholarship, and so she suggests he foreground this aspect rhetorically: 'I think that's a really important thing that you do differently to any one else'. In this way she expands the group's purpose to include skilful articulation of knowledge in a way that matches the norms and expectations of expert research scholarship. This move is bonded rhetorically to the scholarly practice of identifying a 'gap' and positioning oneself vis-à-vis that gap. This is a crucial step for would-be scholars seeking to have their work made public in scholarly publications.

In Excerpt Two, writing group participants can be seen to move between their immediate context (their writing group peers) and a wider community of scholars (Matthew's disciplinary community). In their discussions of each other's writing, group members are concerned not only to understand complex concepts, but also how these should be written about in ways that are valued outside of their own immediate community, by particular kinds of scholars.

Working together to write for others

Writing groups are paradoxical because, on the one hand, they are of themselves discrete communities of scholars, and at the same time they double as places for practising and communicating with other external scholarly communities. These external communities can include supervisors, academic peers, funding panels and the gatekeepers (editors and reviewers) of particular scholarly journals and networks of academic publishing.

The value of writing and talking together simultaneously, for self and for an external audience, is further evidenced in this excerpt from an interview with a writing group participant.

Excerpt Three – Interview

Emily: It's good when other people tell you, like, they don't understand what you're talking about.

Claire: Why is that good?

Emily: Because it means I need to explain it more, like; when I write I know what I'm talking about – but whether everyone else does ...

Claire: But sometimes don't you think 'Well they don't get it 'cause they're just not scientists?'

Emily: Um, yeah but. But yeah, it depends who's going to be reading this ... Some things that people didn't get – well yeah, it's because it was scientific kind of jargon, so it wasn't stuff that I needed to go back and explain – considering who I'm giving it to. So I can, kind of, pick out the bits from what people in the group say, like what needs to be explained and what I think doesn't need to be.

Claire: Terrific. And when you think about the audience of the journal article, does that have any parallels for the audience of a writing group?

Emily: Yeah, in a way, because, ... I suppose it's like the opposite, I don't know who's going to be reading my article. So I would assume that they'd just be kind of like everyone in the writing group, they'd be asking the same kind of questions.

Claire: So it's kind of like, if the writing groups says they don't get it ...?

Emily: Yeah! Then someone else might not get it.

Here Emily, a young science scholar, explains how she deliberately seeks the views of people outside her immediate disciplinary community in order to achieve two objectives: to improve her capacity to better communicate within her own discipline and, importantly, to extend her capacity to communicate with a broader readership.

Because our groups are multidisciplinary, participants are regularly challenged to explain what they're writing about by those from different fields. This review by other student peers from different disciplines can be just as rigorous as review by conference or even journal reviewers – but is more purposefully developmental because the author has the chance to rebut, negotiate and discuss the feedback. It is common to see, through this process of questioning and being asked to explain and clarify meaning, the author return to his or her original text and rework it with a better appreciation of what the readership needs to know.

After a period of belonging to such a group, students often say they can imagine individual group members asking for clarification, critiquing and probing them for specific details: 'I knew you'd ask that!' This familiarity means that they learn to predict the questions their peers would probably raise while they are writing – and they use these internalized voices to help shape their text as they write.

By contrast, students who have had limited experience of others reading and reviewing their writing are less able to predict the kinds of queries, requirements and clarifications that unknown readers may seek. Similarly, doctoral students who show their work only to their supervisor(s) over a period of years may find that their writing can suffer from being too inward looking and decontextualized. As one student remarked: 'Many times I was surprised by the types of issues that had not previously been picked up by my colleagues or supervisor' (Survey respondent, 2007).

Students have different ways of working with what is learnt in a writing group. For example, Emily said she writes down the group's comments during the discussion and then, after the meeting, she collects the written feedback from each of the participants and transcribes all of these comments onto her original draft. She uses this compilation of feedback and her notes from the discussion to rework her text in a way that is powerfully cognizant of her ultimate audience. Doctoral students who participate in our writing groups regularly receive six to eight individual responses, in addition to an hour's discussion of their writing. This provides a rich pedagogical space for the development of writing and publishing know-how.

The writing group is also a forum that supports students throughout the many phases and uses of a piece of writing. As students have been increasingly expected to write papers for conferences during their candidature, more and more of this work is undertaken in our writing groups. Increasingly, we work with students to prepare and rehearse what is originally conceived of as a paper for their College Conference, and which is subsequently brought back to the writing group to be reworked and submitted for publication. Peers learn together experientially through the phases from first draft to submission, review and resubmission.

When students work together over months and years, they witness how writing can serve different purposes and can be altered for different uses. Observing and participating in these processes brings newer students from the periphery to see and participate in real scholarly work at a time and a pace that suits their needs. Like the kind of learning described by Lave and Wenger as 'legitimate peripheral participation' (1991), by seeing, feeling and doing writing as part of a community, these students are learning the real practices of the academy.

In this section I have reviewed the kind of learning that takes place when writing is socially situated and how writing for publication is advanced through the practice of student peer review. This pedagogy of peer review turns on social interaction. The giving, receiving and debating of peer responses to text, creates dynamic spaces for developing writing that is tested and contested, refined, reworked and honed. I now turn my attention to how facilitation contributes to productive writing group pedagogies.

Writing group facilitation as pedagogy

Scenario Two – Writing group tales: 'old hands' and new tricks

As people return to the table with their coffee, conversations, and compliments to Eduardo on his cake baking, we take out our copies of his text. Someone comments about the recent absences of another member and I make a note to myself to email her to see if all's well ... Meanwhile Eduardo reminds the group that this writing is to be submitted to an international journal; he tells us about the journal and its readership, and he explains his aim in the paper.

Over the past 14 months we have seen earlier versions of Eduardo's ideas as they were originally constructed and envisaged in the thesis. Even though none of us are economists, we have developed a working knowledge of Eduardo's research and of his disciplinary norms. 'This is great!'; the first spontaneous comment sums up the unanimous view that Eduardo's writing has improved significantly. In this 5,000-word article, the writing is tighter and there is greater clarity than in those early thesis chapters we reviewed.

Eduardo is writing about familiar content but in an unfamiliar genre – this is his first attempt at a journal article and we have feedback to give him. Comments are made about the slippage between the use of economic jargon and everyday terminology, and the fact that the introduction doesn't yet flow well. Most significantly, the group feels Eduardo should more strongly foreground his central argument and the modelling that he has designed, to validate his contention that he has new knowledge to share. These are matters of positioning and voice rather than content.

Discussion then follows about the discipline-specific use of footnotes versus in-text referencing. It's not long before the focus moves from the technical differences between referencing styles to the very different ways that disciplines regard data and 'evidence'. Given that Eduardo is one of only two group members working within a 'positivist' frame, this kind of this discussion has arisen before. After a while I move the discussion back to the text, explicitly focusing the group's attention on how language is used to show degrees of certainty. In the ten minutes before the meeting closes, I ask people to copy one of the claim statements that appear in Eduardo's paper. I then propose they rewrite it in a way that would be appropriate within their own disciplinary community, using the kind of hedging and modality I'd just spoken about.

All too quickly it's 12 o'clock and someone else is waiting to use the room. We will return in a fortnight.

In this retelling of the second half of our writing group meeting, we see again that learning occurs as peers discuss one person's writing but, in addition, the facilitator is enabling learning. In this example, I, as the facilitator, make specific pedagogical moves. I capitalize on a spontaneous turn in the discussion by taking a particular instance (a claim statement by Eduardo), generalizing it (showing how degrees of certainty are indicated linguistically and their effects) and then particularizing (asking students to rewrite the original claim statement in a way that would suit their own research approach). This is a clear example of the facilitator directing learning; however, not all of the pedagogical work of the facilitator is so obvious.

The kind and extent of facilitation varies according to the maturity and longevity of the group and most especially according to the different needs of its participants. In more formal writing groups with a defined purpose and lifespan, such as those that are part of an undergraduate course or programme, the role of the writing group facilitator is more clearly defined or even prescribed (Speck, 2002). In my experience of writing groups for doctoral students, in contrast, traditional student, teacher and facilitator roles fall away, making facilitation less predictable and less easy to describe.

In this section I am interested in teasing out and analysing the pedagogical practices of successful doctoral writing group facilitation. This is easier said than done. Certainly as I reflect on my own practices, I am aware that some of what I do is simply unique to me or to the particular group that I'm working with. However, there are certain fundamental and transferable practices that I believe are foundational to the success of writing groups for doctoral education. Here I explore these key practices by drawing again from my research and experiences with writing groups.

In the study of writing groups referred to earlier (Aitchison, 2009) we were surprised how frequently participants described 'good facilitation' as a factor that contributed to their learning in writing groups. Broadly speaking, that research showed that a writing group facilitator needs to attend to two different kinds of activities. The first of these is organizational and management practices that facilitate the smooth running and maintenance of the group and thus create a good learning environment. The second set of practices and activities involve direct facilitation of specific learning objectives.

Facilitating a productive environment

In most successful groups the facilitator is responsible for the more mechanical, organizational aspects such as room booking, timetabling, recruitment,
the provision of refreshments, monitoring the writing schedule, group communication and so on. Doctoral students are busy people, often struggling to
balance their student responsibilities and family and professional lives under
considerable pressure. If groups are not well organized with clear communication about meetings, locations and responsibilities, members will quickly
drop away. The sometimes tedious task of ensuring the smooth running of
groups makes a big difference to the success and longevity of writing groups.

I have found that it is important to set and maintain the ground rules and
norms by which the group operates in order to focus and guide participant
practices to maximize effective interaction around writing. In our course-
length writing groups, when all participants start together at the same time,
we negotiate the curriculum and aspects of how we will do, and share, our
writing from week to week. On the other hand, there are some aspects about
the way we wish our groups to work that are not negotiable. We have come
to recognize that it is important at this first meeting to clarify our expectations about processes for participation, commitments to writing, and norms
and procedures for giving feedback.

Establishing and maintaining such group practices in ongoing groups
is rarely so straightforward because members come and go over years and
months. Ideally, as group norms become well established, the facilitator role
diminishes. In Scenario One – 'Writing group tales: the "new girl" learns
the ropes' – some practices have become routine; for example, Marianne
knows the ropes. She gives the group a 'draft history' and nominates the
kind of feedback she wants without being directed. Other practices require
more explicit 'facilitator intervention'. For example, one of the challenges I
faced that morning was to balance the desire of ongoing members for a fair
share of attention to their writing against the need to accommodate a new
member appropriately. In this scenario I illustrated how we introduce new
members by inviting them to talk us through their Table of Contents, thus
introducing their research and routinizing our practices of producing and
discussing text from the outset. At the first meeting I also spend some time
explaining how we operate, reviewing key principles of confidentiality and
the ground rules around giving and receiving feedback on peers' writing. As
backup, handouts are provided.

Other facilitator roles are even less obvious. For example, before Devi
joined the group, she and I had already had a number of email exchanges.
When possible I vet potential new members in order to place them in the
most suitable group according to such criteria as stage of candidature,
research methodology, language proficiency, research focus and discipline. I
email potential new members to find out about them and their work, and to

tell them about our groups. It is also helpful to give the existing group prior notice of a new member's arrival.

Another mechanism for the maintenance of group cohesion and continuity is between-meeting communication. After each meeting I send an email summarizing what occurred at the meeting, confirming who has volunteered text for the next meeting and passing on any other interesting information about group members. This post-meeting email ensures that absent members are kept up to date, acts as a reminder about writing commitments and helps build a sense of community.

As an organizer and manager, the facilitator needs to maintain stability and continuity as well as to ensure that groups are reinvigorated through new membership and new tasks/ideas. Our writing groups are non-compulsory, non-assessable components of the doctoral programme. However, for the benefit of the group and the individual, a certain degree of commitment is necessary and expected. In Scenario Two – 'Writing group tales: "old hands" and new tricks' – I noted for action the absence of a particular member. Balancing students' right to privacy, and their right not to attend, against the group's needs for continuity and cohesion is a difficult task. I believe that the greater the sense of community and belonging, the more likely individual group members are to look out for each other and follow up on members. Over the years of doctoral study, students experience many ups and downs: the stakes are high, research is rarely trouble-free, and even the best student–supervisor relationship involves patches of tension and anxiety. Many students are undertaking higher degree studies at a stage of life when personal, family and community demands are greatest, and some, such as international students, face further social, financial and personal challenges. Added to this are the emotional issues associated with writing itself (Lee and Williams, 1999).

For doctoral students who wish to write for publication, these stresses can be further exacerbated by what appears to be the occluded and mysterious practices of scholarly publication (Casanave and Vandrick, 2003). A writing group can act as a powerful antidote to such stresses, while also being a supportive place for learning about the less clear-cut practices of scholarly publication. The capacity of the writing group facilitator to balance both the learning and the psychosocial needs of members is crucial.

We know that people join writing groups primarily to improve their writing and its output, and for the camaraderie of belonging to a social unit (Ely, Vinz, Downing and Anzul, 1997; Lee and Boud, 2003; Maher *et al.*, 2008; Rankin, 2001). If a writing group facilitator tends to both these desires but prioritizes the learning needs of the group, in my experience negative group dynamics are less likely to become an issue. As one writing group participant said, 'facilitation of the group dynamics, the focus on scholarly values has provided a safe environment where we are able to respect each other and alternate views while developing our own research voice'. It is not uncommon for writing group members to get together after meetings to continue discussions and pursue common research interests. I have observed strong bonds form in some groups where friendships have developed into long-term productive collaborative networks of scholars.

Because learning occurs as peers interact over writing, anxieties about sharing writing need to be addressed sensitively. I have noticed that less confident or reluctant writers may sometimes try to avoid sharing their work, whereas other members may be prolific writers. I try to check and update the group writing schedule at each meeting in order to help ensure a transparent and fair sharing of writing and reviewing opportunities. Participants also use the schedule to set personal writing goals and/or to meet externally imposed deadlines. For example, participants often nominate a series of dates to share and develop their writing leading up to a deadline to submit to a scholarly journal/conference. Many of our participants wouldn't otherwise have opportunities to observe and participate in this kind of writing process over weeks and months towards publication. For them the balance between learning skills for publishing and ongoing peer support, especially through the emotional phases of scholarly journal review, is significant.

Engineering learning

As I have indicated in the writing group tales and excerpts, curriculum focus and pedagogical activity occur spontaneously – for example, in response to a direct inquiry, as an issue arising during the discussion, or from observations on submitted writing. The key point, however, is that facilitator actions originate from, and respond to, what is going on in the group. This just-in-time pedagogical approach to curriculum depends on a high level of facilitator awareness of learner needs, of writing and of writing processes. It also requires a wide repertoire of teaching skills from direct instruction through to negotiated, collaborative, reciprocal engagements.

The amount and the quality of group interaction around writing is influenced by the facilitator. Effective interaction can be achieved in part by attending to the kind of management and organizational tasks outlined above. But in my work with these groups I have also developed a practice of engineering learning by modelling and scaffolding, through direct instruction such as 'mini lessons' and writing tasks, and by directing students to relevant resources and by offering advice.

One of the key areas for my attention as the facilitator is to establish and maintain acceptable practices around giving and receiving feedback (and related issues of confidentiality and trust). Good practices around peer review benefit the novice author and also the peer reviewers, as described by one respondent in an online evaluation:

> It was a bit embarrassing to show my writing to others at the beginning, but after a while this process improved my confidence. The sharing of

our writing was a good method to improve critical analysis, logic and structure of my writing. I learned from the feedback people gave me on my writing but I also learnt from the feedback I gave to other people.

With newer groups I offer my feedback before inviting comments from other group members because this enables me to model how to give feedback, and what kind of feedback is acceptable and productive. In modelling feedback I try to point out the positives first, limit feedback to one or two central points and tie my comments closely to concrete examples in the text. For new groups and with newer members, I often have to do more monitoring of peer feedback, for example modifying, contextualizing or occasionally contesting criticism. As a group matures I am able to pull back, inviting and encouraging comments from others and minimizing my input. In such groups my role becomes one of moderator, synthesizer, co-participant or co-learner.

In the absence of external mechanisms of assessment and compulsion, doctoral writing groups are quite different teaching and learning spaces. The student–teacher and peer relationships are horizontalized (Boud and Lee, 2005), and power and responsibility are diffused, resulting in a more fluid and responsive curriculum and pedagogy. This is apparent in the transcript from the writing group discussion. The distance between 'teacher' and 'student' and 'peer' is narrow, and traditional roles overlap and intermingle. My interactions affirm, encourage, suggest and elicit response, maintain the scope for new thinking/possibilities, and suggest language for describing rhetorical moves. In contrast Matthew's peers are more probing, directive, even critical, as well as encouraging and supportive.

Most of the time the quality and sensitivity of the feedback shared in doctoral writing groups is impressive; however, sometimes feedback can unintentionally become negative or destructive, perhaps through ignorance or over-zealousness. The diversity of research traditions, disciplines and areas of interest, as well as a mix of students of diverse cultural and educational backgrounds, can sometimes contribute to the potential for misunderstanding or misinterpretation. I find this diversity the most challenging and also the most rewarding aspect of working with doctoral writing groups.

Depending on the stage of candidature and of writing, I have come to regard disciplinary differences as one of the most useful pedagogical triggers. I illustrated this in the writing group discussion of Eduardo's work, where I drew attention to the following sentence to illustrate how different practices of language use are employed by particular disciplines:

Improvements in the macroeconomic indicators (see Table 4) to levels reached prior to the financial crisis, explain the recovery of the middle classes which we can see resulted in a reduction in their potential and expectation capabilities.

I used Eduardo's sentence as a prompt to discuss how claims are actioned through the choice of verbs, the use/absence of particular pronouns, the veracity of certain kinds of evidence, the importance of tone and the use of jargon. I then asked students to rework this sentence in a fashion appropriate to their own work, paying attention to the linguistic markers I'd just identi- fied. There isn't always time or opportunity for this kind of activity, but students generally value activities that consolidate and particularize learning to their own purposes.

When participants join a writing group facilitated by an academic litera- cies teacher, they generally look to the facilitator for expertise in language and writing-related matters such as sentence construction, grammar and punctuation. After a while they begin to see that conversations about each other's writing involve bigger issues of academic literacy such as construct- ing an argument, genre, writing processes, voice, identity, power, structure and so on. These realizations can be accelerated for those students writing for publication because the readership and interests are less ambiguous than is the case with a thesis or dissertation. In our groups we ask students writing for publication to tell the group about the readership, style and interests of the journal they are targeting before we give feedback.

When the facilitator's expertise is in language and writing, participants are positioned as the primary 'content' experts, further disrupting traditional student/teacher/supervisory hierarchies. In contrast to student/supervisory situations, in doctoral writing groups, it is the student peers themselves who hold various kinds of expertise and experiences across disciplinary and research fields.

Conclusion

My intention in this chapter has been to explore the affordances that writing groups offer doctoral students wishing to publish during and beyond their candidature. This pedagogical account offers a different perspective on how writing groups actually work to build the kinds of knowledge and practices that equip them to confidently and competently write for publication.

Through scenarios and transcripts of student voices, I have illustrated how students take up the pedagogies of writing groups. When Devi, the 'new girl', joined a community of scholars she engaged immediately in writing for an audience, and she witnessed how Marianne sought from that community review, laughter and debate to help her gain clarity about what she was trying to say and do. We saw in the struggles over Matthew's work how peers actively engage in critique, mirroring the practices of scholarly reviewers and of authors who have to sift through and respond to those reviews. Emily explained why she seeks feedback from her writing group specifically to pre-empt the comments of journal reviews and how she used her peers' reviews to position herself in journal articles. And we saw in the discussion of Eduardo's work how writing changes and improves as authors write and receive feedback over time, honing their ideas and targeting their language for their disciplinary audiences.

The role of the writing group facilitator changes and responds to the circumstances and needs of each group. I have tried to identify and illustrate key practices from my experiences that may help build a more nuanced and robust picture of how facilitation actually works, but still it is easier to say what it isn't. I am not a disciplinary expert, nor am I a mentor, supervisor, assessor or gatekeeper. I do not have any institutionally prescribed or recognized power over doctoral students or over the progress of their candidature. Research writing groups are voluntary associations of peers working collectively to further their own particular project of 'becoming experts' and by making this expertise public. Writing groups work when the facilitator facilitates this objective.

This chapter has described writing groups as vibrant learning environments where pedagogical practices are based on a view of writing as socially situated practice. If research students wish to publish their research, writing groups can provide opportunities for them to do, to watch and to share the literary practices of writing, reviewing and negotiating texts within the community of peers. Writing groups provide students with a safe space to work with peers and a facilitator to 'come to know' their disciplinary and research fields, as well as how to express that knowledge publicly.

Non-compulsory writing groups offer exciting possibilities for doctoral education – but this pedagogy is still new and requires ongoing review and robust empirical investigation so that we can better understand and extend the best aspects to support students' research writing.

References

Aitchison, C. (2003) 'Thesis Writing Circles', *Hong Kong Journal of Applied Linguistics*, 8 (2), 97–115.

Aitchison, C. (2009) 'Writing Groups for Doctoral Education', *Studies in Higher Education*, 34 (8), 905–916.

Aitchison, C. and Lee, A. (2006) 'Research Writing: Problems and Pedagogies', *Teaching in Higher Education*, 11 (3), 265–78.

Boud, D. and Lee, A. (2005) 'Peer Learning as Pedagogic Discourse for Research Education', *Studies in Higher Education*, 30 (5), 501–15.

Casanave, C. P. and Vandrick, S. (eds) (2003) *Writing for Scholarly Publication: Behind the Scenes in Language Education*, Mahwah, NJ: Lawrence Erlbaum Associates.

Cuthbert, D. and Spark, C. (2008) 'Getting a GRiP: Examining the Outcomes of a Pilot Program to Support Graduate Research Students in Writing for Publication', *Studies in Higher Education*, 33 (1), 77–88.

Ely, M., Vinz, R., Downing, M. and Anzul, M. (1997) *On Writing Qualitative Research: Living by Words*, London: Falmer Press.

Galligan, L., Cretchley, P., George, L., Martin-McDonald, K. and McDonald, J.

(2003) 'Evolution and Emerging Trends of University Writing Groups', *Queensland Journal of Educational Research*, 19 (1), 28–41.

Gere, A. R. (1987) *Writing Groups: History, Theory and Implications*, Carbondale: Southern Illinois University Press.

Jones, C., Turner, J. and Street, B. (1999) *Students Writing in the University: Cultural and Epistemological Issues*, Amsterdam: John Benjamins.

Larcombe, W., McCosker, A. and O'Loughlin, K. (2007) 'Supporting Education PhD and DEd Students to Become Confident Academic Writers: An Evaluation of Thesis Writers' Circles', *Journal of University Teaching and Learning Practice*, 4 (1), 54–63.

Lave, J. and Wenger, E. (1991) *Situated Learning: Legitimate Peripheral Participation*, Cambridge: Cambridge University Press.

Lee, A. and Aitchison, C. (2009) 'Writing for the Doctorate and Beyond', in D. Boud and A. Lee (eds) *Changing Practices of Doctoral Education*, London: Routledge, pp. 87–9.

Lee, A. and Boud, D. (2003) 'Writing Groups, Change and Academic Identity: Research Development as Local Practice', *Studies in Higher Education*, 28 (2), 187–200.

Lee, A. and Williams, C. (1999) 'Forged in Fire: Narratives of Trauma in Postgraduate Research Education', *Southern Review*, 32 (1), 6–26.

Lillis, T. M. (2001) *Student Writing: Access, Regulation, Desire*, London: Routledge.

McGrail, M., Rickard, C. and Jones, R. (2006) 'Publish or Perish: A Systematic Review of Interventions to Increase Academic Publication Rates', *Higher Education Research and Development*, 25 (1), 19–35.

Maher, D., Seaton, L., McMullen, C., Fitzgerald, T., Otsuji, E. and Lee, A. (2008) 'Becoming and Being Writers: The Experiences of Doctoral Students in Writing Groups', *Studies in Continuing Education*, 30 (3), 263–75.

Murray, R. (2005) *Writing for Academic Journals*, Maidenhead: Open University Press.

Page-Adams, D. and Cheng, L. C. (1994) 'Establishing a Group to Encourage Writing for Publication among Doctoral Students', *Journal of Social Work Education*, 31 (3), 402–8.

Rankin, E. (2001) *The Work of Writing: Insights and Strategies for Academics and Professionals*, San Francisco: Jossey-Bass.

Richardson, L. (2000) 'Writing: A Method of Inquiry', in N. K. Denzin and Y. S. Lincoln (eds) *Handbook of Qualitative Research*, Thousand Oaks, CA: Sage.

Speck, B. W. (2002) *Facilitating Students' Collaborative Writing*, vol. 28, San Francisco: Jossey-Bass.

Chapter 7

Becoming rhetorical

Rowena Murray

Introduction

Rhetoric is not a subject that doctoral students in every discipline will routinely study. Nor will supervisors universally use the term 'rhetorical' in their discussions of writing with students. The purpose of using the term here is to position centrally the process of learning to write for specific audiences, which is, or should be, an important element of the doctorate.

For the purposes of this chapter, being rhetorical means communicating persuasively in specific rhetorical contexts. Key elements in communication are audience and purpose: being rhetorical involves accommodating a specific audience and choosing a purpose for communicating that is appropriate to that audience. For example, a published article addresses the readers of a specific journal, and has a purpose appropriate for that audience. Rhetorical awareness and skill are essential for researchers if they are to publish their work.

What could, perhaps, be defined as pre-rhetorical writing and thinking can be identified in early doctoral writing: where it overstates the critique of others' work when reviewing literature and methodologies, exaggerates the study's potential contribution to the field, fails to align research aims with outcome claims, misuses specialist terms and uses emotive language. These features of novice writing and thinking may be indicators of rhetorical immaturity, naivety or developing awareness. Doctoral students therefore need to develop rhetorical awareness and perhaps change the way they think about writing in their disciplines.

However, rhetorical knowledge and awareness may not, in themselves, be sufficient. Students also need to develop behaviours that support writing and create psychosocial environments that are conducive to writing. Although rhetorical knowledge is crucial for understanding what journal article writing is about and how to produce it, research shows that successful academic writers adopt specific behaviours, develop specific attributions and build peer relationships around their writing (Hartley and Branthwaite, 1989; Mayrath, 2008). Doctoral students need to learn how to do this too.

Becoming rhetorical is therefore complex, since it works on many levels. Specifically, for doctoral students, it involves learning about the structures of written academic argument, developing a sense of audience requirements, increasing their understanding of how to construct the case for an article's 'contribution' to a field, gaining insights into the politics of academic writing and developing confidence that they have something worth publishing and resilience in dealing with reviews and rejections. At the same time, writing for publication means developing writing practices and networks.

This chapter argues that, although these skills may take time to develop, their development can be initiated at pedagogical events that focus on writing. The pedagogy proposed here is writer's retreat. It provides an exclusive focus on writing and opens up writing to scrutiny, reflection, comparison and review. Moreover, at writer's retreat, doctoral students can try out new writing habits, externalize their existing habits and identify new goals for writing and development.

This chapter draws on a growing literature on writer's retreat (Grant, 2006; Moore, 2003; Murray and Moore, 2006), which suggests that it has distinct benefits for academic writers, including academics engaged in part-time doctorates. The literature provides several models for writer's retreat, but the form of retreat described in this chapter is known as structured retreat, in which participants all write in the same room. A key feature of this 'typing pool' model is that there can be regular discussions of writing-in-progress, discussions that open to scrutiny aspects of writing practice that are often left tacit. It also gives supervisors opportunities to correct misconceptions about academic writing.

Structured retreat was initially developed by me in an Australian setting at a time when research assessment was introduced for the first time. The value of the structured retreat format was that it allowed for information giving and group discussions of presentations to be closely linked to writing. Participants literally wrote their papers around the discussions. This experience suggested that discussion of writing-in-progress – not just feedback on completed drafts – was useful to both developing and more experienced writers, who were struggling to find enough time to write for publication.

This model was then adapted for the faculty in which I now work, where – as elsewhere – there is a growing emphasis on increasing research capacity, output and funding. This faculty has a significant number of academics working on part-time doctorates. Structured retreat was a mode of working that let us have regular discussions about our research aims and writing products, leading to increased research networking. An evaluation study of structured retreat was funded by the British Academy, and this chapter draws on its findings. Quotes from interviews are used to characterize key themes emerging from this evaluation, underscored by feedback from participants, including both academics and doctoral students, at the many structured retreats I have run since that study.

This model of writer's retreat also draws on my experience as a doctoral student in the USA, where, as a PhD student in an English department, I taught rhetoric and composition to undergraduates. This experience raised my awareness of the literature on rhetorical development. It also introduced processes and modes of writing that, although not routinely taught to doctoral students either in the USA or elsewhere, can help them to develop appropriate skills and aptitudes. The purpose of this chapter is to argue that such rhetorical development should be a component of doctoral education. It explores how writer's retreat can be a pedagogy for publishing.

Learning about writing

At retreat students are given information about goal-setting, self-monitoring, pacing, style, structure – all specific to writing for academic journals. Analysis of published writing provides insights into specific styles and structures that are appropriate for the journals that participating students are targeting. There can also be input from expert writers in the discipline, journal editors, reviewers and/or writing experts. Further details on formats and programmes are provided in Murray (2005) and Murray and Moore (2006).

For students, writer's retreat provides an exclusive focus on writing, and the focus of their learning is, uniquely, on the process of learning about writing. Because students are actively engaged in their writing projects at retreat, and because there are regular discussions of what they are writing and how they are doing it, they unpack the processes involved. These discussions expose their developing understandings, their emerging practices and the problems that writing for publication presents for them.

What students think writing for publication involves, how they intend to set about doing it, what they intend to write and what they think and feel about writing for publication as they are doing it are topics worth discussing in specific, individual terms. In some fields, in some departments, this type of discussion is routine, but it is by no means standard doctoral pedagogy. The following sections show that structured retreat is a pedagogy for not only surfacing students' understandings and behaviours but also for reviewing and developing them.

Learning how to get started

> Was having trouble getting started with my article, but having to do it, I got it done.

Starting to write for publication can be intimidating for students. It is a new form of writing, and the stakes are high. Since this is a potential barrier to writing, doctoral students need to learn strategies for overcoming it. Strategies for starting writing are well established (e.g. Elbow, 1973, 1981;

Murray, 2006), but some of these are seen as pedagogies for undergraduate and creative writing, rather than for academic publication. Nevertheless, some of these strategies (freewriting, generative writing and writing to prompts) are introduced at writer's retreat in adapted forms (see Murray, 2005, 2006), and students are prompted to use them at the start of each writing session. They are also asked to set specific goals for each time slot in the programme, and there is discussion about what constitutes an effective writing goal – what might be feasible in, for example, a one-hour session of writing. At the end of each session they review the extent to which they achieved their goals. In this way, they learn to set realistic goals, and they also learn that resetting goals is an important part of goal-setting for writing, since the steps in writing a journal article can be iterative and unpredictable. Students learn what these terms mean, specific to their own writing. This activity is repeated for each time slot, thus providing in-depth experience, observation and reflection on writing goals and the goal-setting process.

Students also discuss what they can do with text produced in this way. Naturally, that text will be in draft form. Revision strategies can be introduced to the discussion and put into practice, or not, depending on the students' goals, needs and priorities.

There is also a group effect. As everyone in the room is writing, so they do start. They are able to forget about the high stakes and focus on generating text. Once they start writing, if they feel like stopping, they force themselves to keep writing until the scheduled break. Knowing that they have to write at retreat prompts participants to do whatever preparation they need in advance of retreat, and this too helps to overcome the 'getting started' barrier. Students often observe that, although they have been unable to write a paper on their own, the structured retreat format enabled them to write immediately. This is perhaps the most important learning benefit of structured retreat, since students who do not overcome barriers to getting started will not produce and submit papers and will therefore miss out on the further lessons they can learn from that process.

Past participants at structured retreat reported that they learned how to make their writing goals specific, to write in defined time increments, to get started more quickly and to keep going more easily. These might seem mechanical outcomes, but they are breakthrough lessons for students. Students also reported that having dedicated time to write journal articles, in an environment where others were doing the same thing, was a major factor in getting started. This shows them 'becoming rhetorical' in the sense that they developed the ability to reduce the 'cognitive load' of writing in order to generate text (Hays and Brandt, 1992: 216); that is, they could move purposefully between their sense of audience and their sense of what they wanted to say.

Learning to learn about writing

> Working together with other academics is very powerful. You're not
> isolated. You see people's way of working.

Not all doctoral students begin their courses or research programmes with all the writing skills they need, although they may feel they should, or may worry that they will be perceived as needing remedial help if they admit to needing further writing development. Perhaps we should make it easier to acknowledge, as happens regularly at retreat, that students and academics continue to learn about writing during the doctorate and even after the doctorate.

This quickly becomes clear to students when academics participate alongside them in retreat and discuss the challenges they face. Again, there is an important group effect, as students realize that they are not the only ones who find writing for publication challenging, that it is, will continue to be, even should be, challenging. This lesson – that they are all in the same boat – is a major shift in their understanding of writing for publication, and it often brings a measure of relief to students.

Whereas students will be familiar with the content and debates in their disciplines' journals, they can benefit from expert analysis of how journal articles are written. At structured retreat, this analysis can focus on how 'research' is created in journals and what they still need to learn about how it is articulated in publications. Although generalized advice on writing for academic journals is useful, advice on writing for the specific journal the student is going to write for is most useful. This type of focused discussion can occur at structured retreat:

- How are articles in [specific journal] structured?
- How are researchers' contributions articulated there? What counts as a contribution in different journals, and how is that stated in, for example, [specific journal's] abstracts, introductions and conclusions?
- What are the [specific journal's] impact factors? Is there a relationship between impact factor and types of research and/or writing?

Such discussion is followed by a writing session, which allows students to put into practice what they learned about writing for their specific target journals. Subsequently, when they review each other's writing, they have an opportunity to further develop these understandings.

They can also debate how knowledge itself is constructed. In practice, some students will be comfortable talking about the politics of writing, but those in the early stages may still expect journal publishing to be neutral, that is free from bias, sexism, nepotism, etc. Some students are initially disillusioned by this discussion. Others become cynical – seeing publishing as just a game. The rhetorical learning that can occur here involves students moving to a position where they can see the field – and journal articles – as a debate and begin to think about how they can establish a position in that debate.

Learning about achieving publication

> This is my third retreat – I always leave at the end with publishable material. Everything I've written here has been published.

During the doctorate, students understandably focus on their research and their emerging thesis. Depending on their contexts and, perhaps, their supervisors, they will be aware of the need to publish, but may find it difficult to prioritize publishing over other tasks. Many academics face the same problem.

At retreat, writing is the sole focus, and this is the main difference between retreat and other student learning environments. This is one of the most valuable features of retreat: writers focus only on the journal article they are writing. Every element of the programme is designed to progress that project. Over time, students learn to develop their own focus on publishing. Those returning for subsequent retreats say that they know better how to prepare to make best use of the structured retreat format. This suggests that there is a learning effect at the first retreat, as participants learn the requirements of this format.

Interviews and informal feedback also show that retreat participants develop an understanding of what is 'publishable'. Successes, and the specific means of achieving them, are shared in discussions. This includes discussions about, for example, dealing with reviewers' feedback, developing specific types of paper or referencing specific research for specific editors or journals, or the pros and cons of 'recycling' papers and ways of doing it. This helps students to understand how they might develop a publishing profile in their fields.

For retreat to be a pedagogical practice, it is important to create moments when students reflect not only on *what* they are writing, but *how* they are writing. This not only helps supervisors keep track of developments, but also helps students articulate and consolidate improvements and, crucially, identify new and/or recurring challenges. Structured retreat allows for these important, regular, brief (10-minute) discussions. In addition, understandings are shared and developed in the many informal discussions during breaks and meals. This underlines the value of making retreats residential, where possible.

For further lessons about writing, students can also look at what productive writers do, although there is little literature on this subject (Hartley and Branthwaite, 1989; Mayrath, 2008; Rymer, 1988). Productive writers who are prepared to share their practices can lead discussion at retreat. A key element in productive writers' careers seems to be disengaging from other tasks and demands in order to write, although the literature does not reveal exactly how they do that, or, more importantly for this discussion, how they learned to do it. The specifics of production are important talking points. Since this discussion is followed by further writing sessions, followed by further discussion, learning can be integrated into students' writing practices.

Learning about research

> Useful to have people in the group from different backgrounds and using different methodologies, lets you see research in its broadest sense, leads to research capacity building and provides research-oriented contacts for return to campus. Plus lots of articles, books and people to follow up later – useful sharing of knowledge. Good to broaden concepts of research out from own areas.

Many doctoral students work in isolation. Some have little or no contact with other researchers. This can be a particular problem for the growing number of part-time students.

Structured retreat is an ideal way of making connections with other researchers and sharing information about research methods and experiences. The experience of talking about research and listening to other researchers in brief discussions helps students to articulate their ideas and develop peer-working skills.

Students can learn a range of lessons from each other about research in this environment: clarifying their understanding of their research and what it involves, extending their epistemological knowledge, adding to their repertoire of different research methods. Implicit in the student quotations I use in this chapter is the development of a researcher identity. Students report that they value the opportunity to both model and practise research and scholarship. Writing at structured retreat facilitates learning about research in context. Some of this learning is spontaneous and unprogrammed but clearly 'capacity building' because of the exclusive focus on writing and the time allocated to writing about research at retreat.

Learning to use feedback

> Very useful to get feedback, write a response to that and then get further feedback and having protected time set aside to do all that.

Students do not always get immediate feedback on their writing. Nor are they always able to act on feedback immediately. They are not always aware of the value of checking their interpretation of feedback. They do not always see the purpose of the iterative process and seemingly endless revisions that may be required in journal writing.

At retreat, feedback is built into brief discussions throughout the programme, and many students print out their papers, sections or abstracts or exchange laptops, so that they can receive feedback. The 'protected' time for writing at retreat means that students can work through the process of receiving and acting on feedback, at least once, and many go through several iterations of the feedback loop as they do multiple revisions. This helps students learn to interpret feedback on their writing and to decide on revision actions. It gives them a way to check their interpretations and get into the habit of checking and revising, as appropriate.

Such feedback practices also prepare students for peer review, and it may take some of the heat out of student–supervisor discussions of writing. More importantly, it shows students the value of putting their writing through the feedback loop, even, and perhaps particularly, in the early stages, with draft abstracts of journal articles, for example. Structured retreat makes clear the value of the iterations in the writing process and helps students to develop the skills of giving, receiving and discussing feedback on their writing.

Learning to use time differently

> Made me realize you can do a lot in a short period of time. Before I would not have thought it was worth starting if I only had one hour.

Students do not always have a good grasp of how the stages in writing for publication can be managed. They are unlikely to know how productive writers manage their time so as to publish regularly. This is one of the most frequently mentioned effects of structured retreat: working within the strictly time-limited programme, in which they are prompted to start and stop writing at specific times, teaches students to structure their writing process differently. It teaches them to write in small amounts of time; but the more important lesson is that they learn to break the complex process of writing for publication into a series of stages that can be done in smaller increments. In other words, students learn, from participating in the retreat's schedule of timed writing slots, that writing journal articles involves a series of steps that they must create for themselves.

This effect may occur immediately, at the first retreat, and may be consolidated at subsequent retreats:

> The more experience you have of writer's retreats the more productive you are, better at using the time, more strategic, more belief in ability to get some writing done. All the retreats have been effective. Repeat-retreat is even more effective.

Retreat provides the framework for this learning. Attending one retreat has an immediate impact on those who attend, and repeat-retreat has an even greater impact.

Learning to do parallel writing

> Working on thesis and book chapter, and getting feedback, was really useful.

Once students start to write for publication, some worry that publishing will distract them from thesis writing. Resubmission, for example, which often requires a quick turnaround, forces students to prioritize publishing, and this can take time away from thesis writing. Even for students doing the PhD by publication, balancing these very different writing tasks is challenging.

Structured retreat allows students to do both. The structured format lends itself to compartmentalization of different writing projects. This also means that, since students have to think in real-time increments, they learn that they can actively shift their focus from one writing project to another: 'As a repeat retreater, learning how to use the time, means I can "park" something that I'm not able to finish here'.

At structured retreat students learn to prioritize and juggle different writing tasks. They are generally writing for publication while they are starting or completing their theses. It is important that they learn how to progress both types of writing at the same time, although this skill is not routinely developed in doctoral programmes. Structured retreat is a pedagogy for developing this important career and life skill.

Learning to be a productive writer

> I would not have done this had I been any place else on the planet. I would never have done this.

Perhaps because the writing for publication process can be quite drawn out, it is unusual for students to experience the feeling of being productive, and yet they have nominally plenty of time to write. This sometimes leads students to form the impression that, no matter how much they do, they are not doing enough.

At retreat, students experience a sense of accomplishment that is new to them. This may be a consequence of having more specific goals and self-monitoring those goals. Retreat provides a different type of experience of writing that is not available in other environments. Clearly, the writers I have quoted will test their assertions in the years to come, but it seems that retreat has shown them how to identify and measure productivity. Measuring their productivity in other terms, including publications, is the subject of important discussions at retreat. Students say they appreciate explicit discussion of different definitions of 'outputs' and 'closures' that shape their writing practices.

Retreat also seems to help students achieve closure on writing that has been started elsewhere: 'Closure on a major piece of work that would not have been possible otherwise'. This reference to 'closure' conveys the writer's sense of the scale of progress made on a major piece of writing. It also demonstrates that structured retreat can be used productively for revising or completing papers begun prior to retreat.

First-time retreat participants generally say that they got much more done than they expected to. They produced more outputs than they thought possible. Serial returners know what they can do at retreat, but report that they still leave with a sense of satisfaction. For students this is an important outcome, as it gives them a sense that they have taken a significant step forward. Although their supervisors will subsequently review their work, it is helpful to work in a context where supervisors are not the primary audience for publications.

Almost every first-time participant suggests that structured retreat is different from any other kind of writing environment. Although it engages them in a novel way of writing, they can also adapt this structure for their own uses. Some returned to the retreat venue alone or with a colleague or partner to run their own 'mini-retreats'. Some used the retreat structure on days when they were writing alone at home. Some used a regular fixed time slot to write a paper in a café. Some used retreat structure for a dissertation workshop they ran for undergraduates, during which they also did some of their own writing. These adaptations suggest that writer's retreat is a pedagogy for publishing, enabling students to develop aptitudes, practices and understandings for publishing.

Structured retreat pedagogy

For structured retreat to be effective, a facilitator has to take responsibility for the pedagogy and for constructive alignment in the retreat curriculum (Biggs, 2003). This involves defining the learning experience of writer's retreat and ensuring that students understand the nature of that learning experience. Students benefit from an explanation about how this experience will enhance their learning and how specific writing tasks will benefit them both in the short term and over the long term.

Introducing the curriculum and pedagogy

The facilitator introduces the theory and practice of writer's retreat, providing an overview of how researchers and academics develop their writing skills to a more advanced level (than in undergraduate curricula) and exploring assumptions, conceptions and behaviours in academic writing. The knowledge, cognitive abilities and skills to be learned are defined, and each student sets learning goals for writer's retreat.

The aims of retreat have to be defined and explanations offered about how the skills of writing for publication differ from the requirements of thesis writing. The activities of retreat also have to be explained to students. These may include developing a writing project, discussing writing-in-progress and trying out new writing practices.

As for any other pedagogy, the facilitator has to support students in preparing for retreat, suggesting appropriate goals, in terms of outputs and processes, describing the retreat programme, answering students' questions and managing expectations. The outcome of preparatory briefing sessions is that each student decides on specific learning goals and intended written outcomes and outputs for retreat.

Students may seek reassurance about the structured programme. Some worry that they will not be able to keep writing for the duration of retreat, whereas others fear that they will not want to stop once they have started. Facilitators explain the goal-setting process, giving examples of effective, specific writing goals. It may be useful for all participants to review their goals, with students and facilitator assessing their appropriateness. The facilitator acknowledges that structured retreat is, in many ways, a new way of writing, but cites evidence of its positive impact. By encouraging students to try it and assess its benefits for themselves, the facilitator reinforces the rationale, while leaving space for discussion and reflection on learning.

Intended retreat outcomes need to be explained and discussed. These might include specific texts, or parts of text, generated and/or revised at retreat, specific writing goals achieved in specific time frames, increased knowledge of other students' – and supervisors' and facilitator's – research and writing and improved understanding of stages in the writing process. Regular discussions throughout the programme allow students to review their progress towards achieving their goals and allow the facilitator to gather information about both achievements and students' ability to self-assess.

The most important preparation task for students is choosing writing projects to work on at retreat, that is deciding on journals – the rhetorical contexts – that they intend to target. The facilitator prompts students to analyse papers published in their target journals, bring instructions for authors, sample papers from the journal and other references, but to do as much preparatory reading before retreat as they can, since most of the retreat day is spent writing. Ideally, students do not have access to the internet at retreat, so as to focus on writing. Although I acknowledge that the internet is a key tool in current academic writing practices – and without wanting to engage in that debate here – lack of internet access does have the benefit of allowing students to focus on their own writing. Students who have participated in this format report that one of its strengths is that it stops them interrupting their own train of thought to add references, for example.

Managing group commitment and involvement

By checking that everyone understands and accepts the retreat's purposes and ground rules, the facilitator establishes commitment and begins to form a positive group dynamic around this new approach to writing. By addressing students' concerns, and reporting on other students' experiences, the facilitator seeks to establish student engagement. However, for students who prefer a more didactic, less discursive model of teaching and learning, this will be a challenge, and the facilitator may choose to adopt a more didactic role by, for example, introducing strategies, providing prompts or suggesting goals at the start of each session of writing.

The facilitator has responsibility for managing student activities. How he or she chooses to play this role is a topic for discussion at either preparatory briefing or introductory discussion at retreat. Throughout retreat, the facilitator works to motivate students to try the retreat mode, monitors the extent to which they are engaging with it and prompts students to measure their progress and development.

During retreat, facilitators will be gathering insights into students' experiences, in informal discussions, planned reflection and observations. At informal discussions during the breaks and in scheduled discussions during the retreat programme, facilitators will be gauging whether students have done the necessary preparation, have grasped the underpinning concepts and are making – or perceive themselves to be making – progress with their writing projects.

A key role for the facilitator is keeping participants to the timetable. For example, during breaks, conversations start up that could run on and cut into writing time. The facilitator has to interrupt these discussions and ask everyone to return to writing. By enforcing the timings the facilitator enables students to develop the discipline of setting real-time goals and keeping to real-time interim deadlines.

Facilitating student activities

The facilitator prompts students' self-monitoring and peer monitoring in brief discussions at the start of writing sessions.

For all brief discussions, the facilitator provides suggestions on talking points and activities for students working in pairs, including mutual review of achievements, goals met, text written and feedback on sections of writing. By listening to students' discussions and observing their interactions, the facilitator monitors activities and outputs informally. Discussion also generates questions and concerns about writing, which the facilitator can then address.

The facilitator can suggest a range of strategies, of which writing to prompts is the most powerful for getting students who run out of steam and/or confidence to start writing again. Suggesting that students end each writing session with a definition of their next writing task, appropriate to the length of the writing slot, helps them to link the different writing sessions and develop momentum. This continuity can be sustained by students developing a more detailed outline than they usually do, which can then be mapped onto the real-time sessions in the retreat programme.

Discussions can be extended to allow students to articulate their thoughts, thus rehearsing content for their writing, and for giving and receiving feedback. By reminding students to give feedback that is appropriate to their peers' target journals, the facilitator reinforces the principles of writing for specific rhetorical contexts. Students need to tell each other about their target journals and how they intend to meet those journals' requirements. Even if students are not familiar with each other's journals, or there are distinct differences between their disciplines, it is useful to ask questions for clarification. In other words, it is *not expected* that they become expert in each other's journals or disciplines; it *is expected* that they prompt each other to define and defend their writing intentions by asking questions. Discussion may also focus on writing-related topics, such as impact factors, citations indices and research assessment processes.

Facilitators play a key role in providing feedback to students and helping them take stock of their progress with writing projects, not only at the end of retreat, but at several points throughout the programme. A particularly important point occurs after the first writing session, in order to gauge students' reactions, provide reassurance, as required, and assist with realistic goal setting for writing at this early stage in retreat. Students often want feedback from someone with more experience of publishing than their peers, and facilitators can provide valuable feedback, for example on a journal article abstract, even if they are not from the student's discipline.

Learning outcomes from retreat

As a result of retreat, students should be able to name and manage stages in the writing process. They should be able to target specific rhetorical contexts. They should be able to articulate the stages in the writing process they are at and describe, implement and review different strategies for working through them. They should be able to evaluate their progress in writing and identify areas for further learning.

While facilitating structured retreat, academics gain insight into the writing processes that students use, challenges they face and strategies that work for them. Facilitators can also progress their own writing. As active participants, they can discuss the challenges they face in their own writing projects, and the challenge of writing at retreat. This dialogue gives students insights into the practices of more experienced writers, and they say they find this both surprising and extremely valuable. They are often surprised that writing can be hard work for experienced writers too. In this way, students learn what writing beyond their first papers might involve. They learn about writing for a range of rhetorical contexts, potentially extending their rhetorical awareness, skills and strategies.

Writer's retreat uses processes that help doctoral students 'become rhetorical' through talking to real audiences (less and more experienced, peers and supervisors), establishing real rhetorical contexts (not virtual or conceptual ones) and learning to structure arguments that are appropriate for that context. Writer's retreat provides a forum for the articulation of these rhetorical dimensions. More specifically, students rehearse potential purposes for their writing, discuss each other's writing-in-progress, give and receive feedback on writing-in-progress, learn to set and reset goals for writing and monitor progress with these writing goals (including giving and receiving feedback on goals).

In addition, writer's retreat provides opportunities for students to extend their rhetorical knowledge, as they cross disciplinary boundaries, learn about methodologies used by other students and learn from experienced, published academic writers. They also learn how to analyse published papers, not only in terms of their content and contribution, but in terms of their rhetorical structures and styles. Facilitators can check whether students are achieving these – and/or other – retreat learning outcomes by using the one-minute paper (Morss and Murray, 2005: 188).

Student learning can be taken a step further when they review their writing practices – during and after retreat – and make changes to those practices, as required. Above all, they can develop confidence that they have something to say to their research communities. They develop confidence in their ability actively to manage both their writing and their development as writers.

Conclusion

Structured retreat is a pedagogy for learning about writing for publication in the course of producing draft papers. It provides a setting where students can be rhetorical and can learn from practice. It also has potential to impact on their understanding of writing, as they discuss multiple interpretations of audience, including real, virtual and conceptualized audiences. In this way students move into what has been called response mode – that is articulating their views to audiences – which is a challenging stage in doctoral learning (Hays and Brandt, 1992: 218).

Structured retreat has a positive impact on students' motivations and attributions, key factors for the long term (Murray et al., 2008), in that it teaches them one way of disengaging from other tasks and demands in order to focus on writing, which has been described as a characteristic of successful academic writers (Mayrath, 2008).

Although other types of retreat are available, structured retreat is a pedagogy that is particularly suited to the needs of doctoral students. Because participants all write in the same room and follow a structured programme, facilitators can manage discussion and monitor students' learning. This would not be possible if students were dispersed in different rooms, writing in solitude. More importantly, structured retreat provides opportunities for students to become rhetorical in the senses outlined in this chapter. As managers of the retreat curriculum, academics can assess the extent to which the format outlined here meets their and their students' requirements and adapt the curriculum as required.

The structured retreat framework outlined in this chapter is supported by other recent research, including a literature review by McGrail *et al.* (2006), which found that the most effective interventions to help academics increase and/or improve their written outputs are *structured* interventions. Structured interventions have helped academics adapt their writing practices in ways that help them increase outputs (Morss and Murray, 2001). Further, writer's group structures, sharing experiences and developing peer relationships are recommended for preparing doctoral students to become independent researchers (Gardner, 2008). All of these types of learning can be built into structured retreat.

In this chapter I have argued that the rhetorical development that occurs at structured retreat should be a component of doctoral education. This argument has implications for writing in campus environments. If the processes involved in writer's retreat are effective, surely there must be a way to transfer them to campus settings in order to sustain their impact? One way is through writers' groups (Lee and Boud, 2003; Murray and MacKay, 1998; Murray and Moore, 2006). This argument also has implications for supervisors. Helping students to become rhetorical does not require supervisors to be writing teachers, but supervisors can help by routinely shifting the focus to writing. Although writing is seldom the sole focus as it is at writer's retreat, arguably writing should be given greater focus more often, if it has these learning benefits.

Finally, becoming rhetorical means making choices about audience and purpose, and structured retreat provides an environment where students can not only write but also rehearse their rhetorical choices. Structured retreat puts students in charge of their writing: they have to make choices and decisions at every stage in the writing process. It teaches them to manage the different levels of decision. Perhaps more importantly, it teaches them to learn through discussion of and feedback on writing-in-progress.

Acknowledgement

I would like to acknowledge the insightful and helpful feedback I received – at writer's retreat – on a draft of this chapter from Kathy Harrington and

Peter O'Neill and to thank the British Academy for funding the study on which this chapter draws.

References

Biggs, J. (2003) *Teaching for Quality Learning at University*, 2nd edn, Buckingham: Society for Research into Higher Education.

Elbow, P. (1973) *Writing without Teachers*, Oxford: Oxford University Press.

Elbow, P. (1981) *Writing with Power*, Oxford: Oxford University Press.

Gardner, S. K. (2008) ' "What's Too Much and What's Too Little?": The Process of Becoming an Independent Researcher in Doctoral Education', *Journal of Higher Education*, 79 (3), 326–51.

Grant, B. (2006) 'Writing in the Company of Other Women: Exceeding the Boundaries', *Studies in Higher Education*, 31 (4), 483–95.

Hays, J. N. and Brandt, K. S. (1992) 'Socio-cognitive Development and Student Performance', in M. Secor and D. Charney (eds) *Constructing Rhetorical Education*, Carbondale: Southern Illinois University, pp. 202–29.

Hartley, J. and Branthwaite, A. (1989) 'The Psychologist as Wordsmith: A Questionnaire Study of the Writing Strategies of Productive British Psychologists', *Higher Education*, 18, 423–52.

Lee, A. and Boud, D. (2003) 'Writing Groups, Change and Academic Identity: Research Development as Local Practice', *Studies in Higher Education*, 28 (2), 187–200.

McGrail, R. M., Rickard, C. M. and Jones, R. (2006) 'Publish or Perish: A Systematic Review of Interventions to Increase Academic Publication Rates', *Higher Education Research and Development*, 25 (1), 19–35.

Mayrath, M. C. (2008) 'Attributions of Productive Authors in Educational Psychology Journals', *Educational Psychology Review*, 20, 41–56.

Moore, S. (2003) 'Writers' Retreats for Academics: Exploring and Increasing the Motivation to Write', *Journal of Further and Higher Education*, 27 (3), 333–42.

Morss, K. and Murray, R. (2001) 'Researching Academic Writing within a Structured Program: Insights and Outcomes', *Studies in Higher Education*, 26 (1), 35–52.

Morss, K. and Murray, R. (2005) *Teaching at University: A Guide for Postgraduates*, London: Sage.

Murray, R. (2005) *Writing for Academic Journals*, Maidenhead: Open University Press.

Murray, R. (2006) *How to Write a Thesis*, 2nd edn, Maidenhead: Open University Press.

Murray, R. and MacKay, G. (1998) 'Supporting Academic Development in Public Output: Reflections and Propositions', *International Journal for Academic Development*, 3 (1), 54–63.

Murray, R. and Moore, S. (2006) *The Handbook of Academic Writing: A Fresh Approach*, Maidenhead: Open University Press.

Murray, R., Thow, M., Moore, S. and Murphy, M. (2008) 'The Writing Consultation: Developing Academic Writing Practices', *Journal of Further and Higher Education*, 32 (2), 119–28.

Rymer, J. (1988) 'Scientific Composing Processes: How Eminent Scientists Write Journal Articles', in D. A. Joliffe (ed.) *Advances in Writing Research*, Vol. 2: *Writing in Academic Disciplines*, Norwood, NJ: Ablex, pp. 211–50.

Chapter 8

Mentoring doctoral students towards publication within scholarly communities of practice

Amanda Haertling Thein and Richard Beach

Introduction

In this chapter, we describe the experience of a professor/doctoral advisor (Richard) mentoring his doctoral advisee (Amanda) on how to publish academic research. We demonstrate that preparing doctoral students to publish in top-tier journals involves more than simply providing them with advice on rhetorical strategies or genre conventions for writing research. Doctoral students often need mentoring that assumes that academic writing and publishing is, as Kamler and Thomson (2008: 508) note, 'text work/identity work', in that 'texts and identities are formed together, in, and through writing. The practices of doctoral writing simultaneously produce not only a dissertation but also a doctoral scholar'. This means that mentoring involves constructing:

> A space in which both doctoral researchers and supervisors are learning selves in transition. This is a social and relational space in which performance (experience, dialogue, writing) allows the dynamic 'smudge' of learning, the movement from one knowing-being to another. In text work and identity work, writing is performance.
>
> (Kamler and Thomson, 2006: 19)

Unfortunately, doctoral students often receive little effective mentoring to support this repositioning of identity (Nettles and Millett, 2006). As a result, many doctoral students never complete their dissertations – certainly for multiple reasons, but a primary one being ineffective mentoring (Ehrenberg, Jakubson, Groen, So and Price, 2007; Golde and Dore, 2001; Lovitts, 2001). Or, if they do complete their dissertation, they never publish any articles from that dissertation (Lovitts, 2001).

Redefining oneself as a publishing 'scholar' involves developing a sense of agency and self-confidence in the belief that one can contribute new knowledge to their field. Mentoring doctoral students and beginning assistant professors to develop that agency and self-confidence requires helping them address the challenges of over-committing, perfectionism, procrastination, disorganization, lack of motivation, and choosing performance-debilitating circumstances – issues that often have more to do with acquiring new social practices and dispositions than with acquiring academic skills.

Richard mentored Amanda not only by providing her with advice on how to cope with these challenges, but also by involving her in collaborative research and co-publishing experiences through which she acquired the self-confidence associated with publishing academic work. Thus, Richard's mentoring, as is the case with effective teaching, was as much about designing and scaffolding active participation for Amanda in a community of practice as it was about doling out advice to her. And, because Richard and Amanda collaborated on various research and publishing projects, the advice that he did provide to her was contextualized within her engagement in these projects, thereby making that advice relevant to acquiring certain practices.

Through this participation, Amanda actively learned about the roles, practices and norms operating in institutional or academic 'activity systems' constituting academic publishing. And, through her active engagement in co-publishing, she repositioned her identity and agency as a 'published scholar' within new communities of practice (Holligan, 2005).

Cultural-historical activity theory (CHAT) learning theory provides a useful framework for identifying how these competing demands are grounded in institutional forces (Engestrom, 1987; Russell, 1997; Russell and Yanez, 2003), as well as for understanding what motivates people to engage in certain communities. CHAT learning theory posits that learning involves acquiring tools associated with achieving certain objects or outcomes in a community or system, objects defined as those concerns or interests that drive participation in any activity (Engestrom, 1987).

Developing a driving sense of purpose for being in a doctoral programme is essential for success in completing the programme, particularly at the dissertation stage (Ehrenberg, Jakubson, Groen, So and Price, 2007). When Richard first met Amanda, he was struck by the fact that she had a clear sense of purpose for what she wanted to study and accomplish, related to students' responses to multicultural literature, a focus she derived from teaching high school English in a suburban Denver school. Amanda was particularly interested in studying issues of gender differences related to female students' literacy responses:

> I became interested in the gendered aspects of reading and responses practices that girls engage in outside of the classroom and how understanding these practices might shed light on stances girls take toward literature read in the classroom. My interest in knowing more about the gendered culture in this community and in learning about the intersection of inside and outside reading and response practices led me not only to my dissertation topic, but also to theoretical and empirical readings that helped me to acquire a new academic discourse that I needed

for understanding gender – a discourse related to critical feminist perspectives.

What's important here is that Amanda's object coincided with Richard's own object – his strong interest in exploring how responses to competing perspectives and social worlds portrayed in multicultural literature serves to foster students' understanding of the complexities of their own social worlds (Beach and Myers, 2001; Beach, Appleman, Hynds and Wilhelm, 2005). Sharing the same common objects around studying students' responses to literature meant that they were mutually engaged in supporting each other in their collaborative work. Amanda explains:

> My dissertation topic was related to Richard's primary area of inquiry in that it involved socio-cultural aspects of response to literature. It was directly tied to the research Richard and I had conducted earlier in as much as it developed from questions about gender that grew out of our initial research. However, I also developed a new area of inquiry in my dissertation by studying both out-of-class reading practices in addition to the classroom practices I had studied with Richard. My topic allowed me to draw heavily on the theory and knowledge I learned from my work with Richard, but also challenged me to investigate new avenues of inquiry and theory.

CHAT also defines how activities are part of larger systems defined by roles, norms and a sense of community (Engeström, 1987).

Competing activity systems of the doctoral programme

In participating in the doctoral programme, Amanda was engaged in a number of different competing systems – the systems of teaching, graduate school dissertation requirements, and job market (Lundell and Beach, 2003). Each of these systems is driven and constituted by different roles, norms and a sense of community associated with achieving different objects/outcomes. Richard's mentoring of Amanda therefore required addressing a range of different systems driven by different objects/outcomes.

Teaching

Amanda placed a high priority on her teaching as a teaching assistant of methods courses in Richard's English education teacher education programme. She was driven by her desire to model effective instruction to her pre-service and in-service teachers.

The challenge for many doctoral students is how to balance their work as a teaching assistant with their research and writing, particularly for students who, like Amanda, wanted to teach at a 'research university' that places a high priority on research and publications as requirements for tenure (Beach and Thein, 2009; Prior and Min, 2008).

Knowing that Amanda wanted to obtain a position at a 'research university', Richard frequently shared his own experiences with her about balancing the demands of research and teaching in his work at the University of Minnesota. He stressed that the two need not be mutually exclusive: that the object of effective teaching – engaging students in active learning – often involves research methods of facilitating discussions or interviewing. He frequently shared his research experiences with his pre-service and in-service teachers to model ways of conducting their own teacher action research or literary response/media ethnography studies (Beach, 2004):

> From the start of my work with him, Richard encouraged me to see teaching and research as linked, arguing that his best teaching often arose from his own research interests. I took this advice seriously, not only bringing experiences from my research into my teaching of methods courses, but also developing a course on teaching multicultural literature – a course that grew out of my research interests and one that my research led me to believe was much needed. I taught two iterations of this course at the University of Minnesota and then continued to revise and teach this course at the University of Pittsburgh. Because it is so deeply connected with research that I think is critically important in the field of English Language Arts, it continues to be both the class that I enjoy most and the class brings me the highest ratings from students.

The graduate school dissertation requirements

The second system facing doctoral students are the specific genre rules or conventions constituting dissertation writing required by their university's graduate school, rules or conventions that may vary across different units within a university. In 2005, the Graduate School at the University of Minnesota required the production of a single print document; it was also expected within Richard's department that a research dissertation be organized according to the sections of statement of the problem, research review, methods, findings and discussion/implications for further research/teaching.

The challenge for doctoral students wanting to publish separate research reports from their dissertation is how to translate their dissertation into more focused, shorter journal-length reports (since 2005, the Graduate School at the University of Minnesota provides students with the option of writing several research reports in lieu of a single dissertation). Whereas the dissertation genre entails making explicit in extensive ways one's methodological approaches, assumptions and explanations of findings to serve the object of demonstrating a student's research competency, the journal research report involves a more truncated, focused version of one's methods and findings.

Brent Kilbourn (2006: 531) explains that dissertation writing requires a student to be:

> self-conscious [which] tends to reflect the layers and complexity of the process of a dissertation as it unfolds from conceptualization to finished product. But more significantly, self-conscious method is the means for justifying the various moves that are made within all the other qualities expected of a doctoral dissertation, from conceptualization to literature review, to argument, to form. And here, perhaps, we can see the rough distinction between research in general and research done within the rubric of a doctoral dissertation. A doctoral dissertation is, after all, not only a piece of original research; it is a demonstration that the candidate is ready to do independent research.

In mentoring Amanda about adopting these dissertation genre conventions, Richard stressed that, although she needed to 'follow the rules' in writing the dissertation, ultimately she would be transforming the dissertation, as described later in this chapter, into articles.

The job market

The third system influencing doctoral students' academic publishing is the job market. In today's competitive job market, particularly for positions at research universities, students need to graduate with résumés listing conference presentations and publications, evidence that they have the ability to produce scholarly work necessary for obtaining tenure, given the fact that search committees are reluctant to hire assistant professors who may not obtain tenure and risk the possibility of losing a position. When mentors proactively encourage publication during students' programmes, students are more likely to publish (Heath, 2002; Kamler, 2008).

Richard stressed to Amanda the importance of using presentations and publications to position herself in the job market so that she would be 'known' as having her own original, particular research focus or agenda that would appeal to potential employers. Richard's paradox of being a mentor is that, although he wanted Amanda to acquire and adopt his particular beliefs and ideas, he also wanted her to develop her own independent perspectives, independence associated with autonomy, self-motivation and self-direction as a valued goal of doctoral programmes (Gardner, Hayes and Neider, 2007).

Amanda was also aware of this paradoxical positioning and the need for her to develop her own identity as a scholar:

> As I considered my dissertation topic, I found myself pulled in two directions. First, I felt fortunate to have worked with Richard, who is a nationally-recognized leader in my field, and I knew that much of my

early reputation as a scholar would be based on my status as his advisee. Moreover, I expected that when I applied for my first job, people would anticipate that my research agenda, knowledge-base and theoretical stance would in some way be aligned with Richard's. Likewise, I clearly did have a great deal in common with Richard as a scholar given that I chose to study with him in the first place and given that I was deeply entrenched in a two year research project with him.

However, it was also clear to me that the people I met in my job search would want to see that I was capable of independent thinking and scholarship. Without this quality I certainly wouldn't be a likely candidate for success in the tenure stream. No matter how much personal initiative I took on my collaborative work with Richard, I knew there were those who wouldn't see me as my own scholar until I developed a separate line of research. Ultimately I chose a dissertation topic that seemed a natural yet clearly divergent extension of the work I had previously conducted with Richard.

Four mentoring practices

To mentor[1] Amanda's publishing within the context of these systems, Richard employed four practices: mutual engagement in collaborative research; co-authored research; reciprocal review and evaluation; and networking.

Mutual engagement in collaborative research

One major problem with academic mentoring is that a busy faculty may not devote the time necessary to meeting regularly with students to foster relationships that lead to mutual trust and respect (Mullen, 2005, 2007). Although 85 per cent of the students in one study were satisfied with the quality of their mentoring, the level of their satisfaction was related to the frequency of regular meetings with their mentor, as well as the quality of those meetings – for example, the extent to which their mentor was prepared for a meeting (Heath, 2002). This ongoing interaction with mentors represents what Prior (1994, 1998: 101–2) described as 'deep participation' of students with mentors, which differs from the experience of graduate students merely 'passing' through their programmes by simply completing assignments.

Amanda was a full-time student, and for one year of her programme was supported by Richard as a research assistant to work with him on a year-long study of high school students' responses to multicultural literature. This study served as the basis for her dissertation (Thein, 2005), as well as co-authored conference presentations, journal articles and a book (Beach, Thein and Parks, 2007). In this study, Amanda's job was to collect data from the classroom they were studying through observations and interviews.

Because Amanda and Richard were working together on this project, they were continually sharing decisions, not only about research methods and data analysis, but also about how to present and publish their work.

To create this reciprocal relationship, Richard emphasized the fact that their decisions about research and publishing were collaborative – that Amanda had equal say in this work and that he valued her input. Participating in this co-equal partnership served to reposition Amanda's identity from that of 'student' to 'co-researcher' and 'co-author' whose decisions were going to affect the quality of the research and whether their work was going to be published.

In this collaborative project, Amanda also acquired expertise in conducting ethnographic analyses of community and school cultures, leading her to make theoretical and empirical connections between certain class and gender discourses in the community and students' responses to literature. As she notes:

> Although my study with Richard was initially planned as a classroom ethnography of students' responses to multicultural literature, I initiated a new phase of data collection in the second semester of the study driven by my desire to understand the cultural practices and norms operating in the working-class high school. I conducted field observations of a variety of classrooms, several lunch periods, athletic events, and a student assembly, as well as writing general observations of the hallways during passing periods and physical descriptions of the building. I also observed other classrooms, taking field notes in which I observed the nature of the students' social interactions in class discussions. I ultimately linked discourses found in the school and community with students' responses to multicultural literature in the English classroom. For instance, given the school's storied history as a football and hockey powerhouse, a primary discourse that we found to be operating in the school and community was one that we deemed a 'discourse of athleticism.'

Through developing this expertise, Amanda as a collaborator was providing original, significant interpretations of the study results, something that Richard appreciated as complementing his own interpretations.

Co-authored research

Richard also mentored Amanda by co-publishing research with her. Through this collaboration, he modelled his own practices involved in conducting research and publishing that he had acquired over a 35-year period. Based on her experiences with Richard, Amanda then continued to publish not only on her own, but also as a co-author and mentor with her own graduate students in her first years as an Assistant Professor at the University of Pittsburgh.

In preparing submissions to certain journals, Richard shared with Amanda his perspectives on the expectations and biases of particular editors and potential reviewers related to acceptance decisions as well as requests for revisions. He noted that, for example, certain editors and reviewers bring particular interests and disciplinary orientations that shape their editorial judgements as to what constitutes original, ground-breaking scholarship worth publishing. Within any disciplinary fields, there are debates on issues of valid research methods and theories. In framing research reports, it is critical to include references to these debates to demonstrate one's awareness of them. For example, in their work, Richard and Amanda were using critical discourse analysis (CDA; Gee, 1996) and critical race theory (Bonilla-Silva, 2001) to identify discourses of race, class and gender shaping high school students' literary responses. In applying these approaches, Richard noted that it was important to point out differences between approaches such as CDA and critical race theory, which examine issues of race, class and gender difference as shaped by institutional forces, and other more individualistic perspectives, for example those that perceive perceptions of race as simply a matter of individual prejudice or attitudes (Bonilla-Silva, 2001).

Engaging in collaborative writing requires that co-authors agree who will contribute what material so that authors are equally responsible and accountable for completing their work (Ede and Lunsford, 1990). In working on their co-authored book on high school students' responses to multicultural literature (Beach, Thein and Parks, 2008), along with another author, Richard, Amanda and Daryl developed an outline delineating which author was responsible for reporting certain results. They also developed an internal review plan for giving feedback on each other's contributions.

Reciprocal review and evaluation

Richard's most significant mentoring practice involved providing feedback to Amanda in ways that modelled strategies for self-assessing her independent publishing based on uses of rhetorical strategies involved in academic publishing. For Amanda, translating her dissertation into one or more reports from it, including a report to submit for the Promising Researcher competition sponsored by the National Council of Teachers of English (NCTE) (an award she eventually received), proved to be a challenge.

Mentoring students in translating their dissertation into journal articles involves helping them summarize their review, methods and results to fit the journal article genre. Amanda learned how to pull out parts of her 292-page dissertation into shorter pieces from working with Richard on book chapters, articles and conference proposals:

It is tempting to see a dissertation as a manuscript that tells one, very thorough story. As a student and now as an assistant professor, I've read any number of article-length or even book length manuscripts that are clearly a condensed version of someone's dissertation. While such work is important, particularly in its depth, I learned from Richard that any large set of data is likely to have more than one story to tell. Therefore, rather than summarize my dissertation, my efforts in publishing from it have been directed toward identifying the most significant and relevant findings and selecting and analyzing focused sets of data from my dissertation that support those findings in journal-length manuscripts. For instance, while I focused on all of the female students in one classroom, and seven students in particular, I have written two manuscripts that are case studies of individual students. In each of these manuscripts I found that focusing on one student allowed me to write with the kind of depth and detail that I came to value through my ethnographic methodological framework, while also allowing me to make concise, careful arguments that were relevant to the field.

In my current work as an Assistant Professor, I encourage the doctoral students I work with on my research to carve out pieces of our larger data set and to take the lead on developing manuscripts that they think make compelling and concise arguments that journals will want to publish.

Richard assisted Amanda in this process by providing feedback to her NCTE Promising Researcher report that stressed the need to focus the summary of the related research to make the rhetorical case for the value and significance of her study. He noted that, in translating dissertations into articles, students often devote too much space in an article to a lengthy review of related research – a common feature of the dissertation – without focusing that review on building the case for the value of their study.

For example, in her research review in a draft of her dissertation study on female high school students' identity constructions (Thein, 2005), Amanda noted:

> Being a 'popular female' requires the construction of a figured world of romance that defines those practices contributing to being 'popular'. And because social worlds are continually evolving through cultural and historical shifts, so the self as constructed in and by these worlds is continually evolving and changing in ways that are mediated by these cultural and historical shifts.

Richard responded with this suggestion: 'Make a specific link to the need for research on how figured worlds shape female identity construction – to build the case for your study'. This response is designed to encourage Amanda to use the research review to argue for the value of her particular study.

In her review, Amanda also argued for the need for research on:

> the dynamic ways high school girls take up social and cultural discourses
> and literacy practices in negotiating their identities and in constructing
> their stances and responses to diverse literature. Such research may yield
> implications for choice of classroom texts and pedagogical practices in
> teaching literature that may be more equitable and more encouraging of
> critical engagement for all students.

Richard responded with the suggestion: 'connect this more specifically to
your particular research topics and questions – you may be repeating stuff
again at the end of Chapter 3, but that's part of the genre'. In this response,
Richard notes the need for Amanda to assess whether her discussion relates
directly to her research questions.

In describing her results, Amanda noted that a classroom she studied
seemed to lack open, critical expression:

> While this initial glimpse into Deanna's classroom suggests a space with
> little room for agency, critical thinking, or creative expression, a closer
> look suggests that this was not always the case. At Thompson High
> School, Deanna's classroom was in many ways a progressive, creative,
> and even critical environment.

Richard responded: 'Emphasize the idea that given the larger school culture,
her class was relatively progressive – I wonder if you could note any observations of any other classes that were even more authoritarian'. In doing so,
he is inviting Amanda to employ a central research strategy of comparison
– defining the relative progressive nature of Deanna's classroom by comparison with other classrooms – adopting the role of 'researcher' who seeks
understanding through comparison.

He also pushed Amanda to adopt alternative critical perspectives. For
example, Amanda describes students' discussions of a scene from Toni
Morrison's *Beloved* in which the characters Halle and Sethe have sex in a
cornfield:

> Many students came to class confused not only about thematic issues
> in the text, but also about basic plot points. Many students in class
> expressed shock and embarrassment in not understanding the 'cornfield
> scene.'

In response to a transcript of this discussion, Richard shared his own
interpretation:

There's something else going on here that's a part of a gendered space involving overlapping/interruptive speech which may or may not be associated with certain genders, but is a feature of adolescents' talk. There's a debate on this – part of avoiding the essentializing of talk by gender. The key idea is that the ideas constructed are perceived to be a collaborative group effort versus just individual efforts (Cameron, 2007) – maybe associated with female gender practices??

In providing his own interpretation of the discussion data, Richard provides an alternative framing of the data – that the students' interruption/overlapping is a gendered phenomenon. He's also qualifying his framing that this gender perspective may be problematic if it reifies an essentialist perspective on gender differences. Because Amanda knew that Richard was continually challenging essentialist approaches to gender differences, she knew 'where he was coming from' and accepted his feedback to make further revisions.

At the same time, as part of their co-publishing, Amanda provided feedback to Richard's writing, thereby learning to position herself as both a teacher and a colleague. In their initial co-publishing, Amanda focuses on issues of grammar/syntax editing. For instance, Amanda rephrased the following few sentences in a book chapter to clarify Richard's meaning:

Original phrasing:
 Another possible explanation for the lack of awareness of a discourse of Whiteness is that these students perceive themselves as 'urban' as distinct from suburban white students and relatives whom they accuse of harboring racist attitudes. For example, they cite instances in which their relatives voice racist comments, particularly about their urban world. By distinguishing themselves from these suburban Whites as distinct from themselves as urban Whites, they then assume that they are not racist.

Amanda's comment:
 Richard, I think the last sentence needs rewording for clarity. How about, 'By distinguishing themselves from suburban whites whom they view as ignorant and racist, urban whites may assume that their membership in a racially diverse "urban community" automatically defines them as knowledgeable about diversity and being "non-racist"'?

As Amanda became more comfortable in her role as a collaborative author, she focused more on larger issues of content and organization. For example, in responding to a draft of chapter for their book, Amanda suggested reorganizing the chapter:

 Richard, it seems to me that we might not need to explain the model of inquiry-based education until we get to the Crosswinds example. I would suggest cutting those pieces from this section, and renaming this section to reflect a focus on place-conscious education as a space for exploring dialogic tensions. I would suggest that we don't mention Crosswinds or the inquiry model until the actual section on Crosswinds. I'll make the changes here. You can just delete them if you don't think it works.

In other cases Amanda drew on her emerging skills as an interpretive researcher to offer alternative perspectives on Richard's analyses of data. For example, Richard wrote about how many of the students in their study devoted long hours of time in the workplace, a function of their being working-class:

> Workplace. This is a neighborhood with a storied history of work. While the glory days of manufacturing have long passed, the trait of a strong work ethic merges with the emphasis on athletics in such a way that it comes to signify the 'Thompson Tradition' that is emphasized and emblazoned in the buildings and discourses within this community.
>
> This message must have resonated through many homes in the area given the high percentage of employment among the students in our study: nearly 80 percent of the students in our study work in addition to their high school studies and extracurricular activities. Of these students, several average more than 30 hours a week at their jobs, with the median being closer to 12 hours per week. Given the lower socio-economic status of the community, the majority of students who are employable indeed work part-time jobs.

Amanda challenged this interpretation and offered an alternative interpretation:

> Richard, work among students at Thompson doesn't sound much different to me from work among suburban students. In my experience (I have no stats on this) most suburban students work some amount after school or on weekends. Most of them also work for minimum wage with no benefits, etc. They, too have no skills at this point in life. I'm guessing that the real difference is what the money they make is used for. For most suburban students it's probably spending money or money to pay for something like their car insurance or gas for their car. It's also clearly a temporary, high school job that will end when they finish school. For urban kids at Thompson, this money may go toward household expenses, rent, etc. and may be part of their obligation to their families. Also jobs that these students work during high school may end up being long-term jobs following high school. So maybe we should rethink this section?

In questioning whether students' work is simply a function of being in a working-class school, Amanda is suggesting that Richard needed to consider differences in the purposes for which students work – that, whereas students in working-class schools work to support their families, students in suburban schools are working to acquire spending money. This led to his revising his text to make that point.

Networking

Although graduate students and beginning assistant professors may be highly effective writers, they also need to know how to participate with and engage audiences. That participation itself serves to develop their identities as published scholars. Holligan (2005: 271–2) cites the example of a student, Anne, who had little interaction with her peers, and therefore did not have a chance to 'discover where her academic strengths lay and through social comparison learn how to share difficulties and academic challenges'. He also noted that Anne was overly deferential to and accepting of authoritative positions. To foster more social interactions and the adoption of a critical stance, Holligan involved Anne with a group of researchers who collaboratively conducted research, attended conferences, wrote papers and participated in bi-weekly meetings. He noted that 'by debating her research ideas at supervisory and external meetings, Anne's awareness of the role of argument in relation to understanding and interpreting data was bolstered. Networking through conferences and seminars gave her access to a community committed to research'. He also noted that, through grappling with competing theoretical perspectives applied to data, she began to adopt her own voice, moving away from her deferential orientation.

Richard's mentoring also involved helping Amanda learn to promote her work and voice through socializing her into relevant professional communities of practices, based on the idea that moving into an academic field involves not only what you know but also who you know (Wenger, 1998). He encouraged Amanda to engage in networking by attending and speaking at national conferences as important spaces for becoming known in the field, but for meeting potential employers. Attending and presenting at conferences also provided Amanda with insights into how scholars develop their ideas and talk about their research in progress (Cobb et al., 2006; Kamler and Thomson, 2006). Amanda reflects on her learning experiences at conferences:

> Conferences and meetings gave me opportunities to share my work with people whose work I admired. I was surprised to find that these people did not always have all the answers and that they took my work very seriously. These events afforded me the opportunity to get to know other doctoral students and junior faculty members from across

the country – some of whom are now both my friends and well-known scholars in my field – who were typically eager to share their experiences with me and to offer me advice. All of these experiences were critical in my development of an identity as a scholar, not just as a student. They were also key experiences in helping me gain proficiency in the genre of academic social interaction – a genre that became very useful in on-campus job interviews.

Presenting research at conferences was one of the most important aspects of my preparation for the job search. During the first three years in my doctoral program I presented many times with Richard. During my final year I independently proposed and presented my dissertation research at several national conferences. For me the transition between presenting with Richard and presenting my own research felt very significant. It was proof to me that I could independently participate in this discourse community of which I had worked so hard to become a member.

Participation in national organizations and conferences helped me find my place in the field of Literacy education. This sense of place grounded my academic identity as I 'marketed' myself in my job search. Having a solid idea of who I was and who I was becoming as an academic helped me to apply for positions that were best suited for me; it also helped me to be savvy in determining whether particular schools and departments would fit well with my interests.

It should also be noted that Richard was not Amanda's only mentor. He encouraged her to build relationships with other mentors so that she was supported by a range of different faculty members about publishing practices, including by Professor Carol Berkenkotter, with whom she took a course on critical ethnography and with whom she co-authored a book chapter (Berkenkotter and Thein, 2005) on conducting institutionally organized social practices:

> In working with Dr. Berkenkotter I learned how pieces of research from different theoretical backgrounds can be combined in meaningful ways in publishable academic writing. Although my research was grounded in theories of 'cultural models' (Gee, 1996), and Dr. Berkenkotter's focused on genre theory and genre knowledge (Berkenkotter and Huckin, 1995), we had in common an interest in discourse analysis and ethnography. The chapter we co-wrote ultimately combined ethnographic descriptions from Dr. Berkenkotter's work in a upper-middle class, suburban, private elementary school with my work in a working-class, urban, public high school – two seemingly disparate contexts – to construct a compelling argument about ways that institutional spaces serve to construct social

practices. Collaborating with Dr. Berkenkotter helped me to understand the productive and publishable nature of interdisciplinary scholarship.

Later, as an Assistant Professor at the University of Pittsburgh, Amanda received further mentoring from a number of her colleagues. She explained some of the key moments in that mentoring:

As an Assistant Professor at the University of Pittsburgh, I learned much about academic publishing. During my first years at the University of Pittsburgh I wrote my first single-authored, full-length research articles. Several senior colleagues in my department volunteered to read my articles and help me prepare them for publication. Perhaps the most useful advice I got was from a colleague in a field very different than mine. Reading one of my articles without disciplinary expertise, this colleague was able to point to places in my article where I needed 'guideposts'; to remind my reader of the argument I am making and to help the reader navigate the different sections of my paper. He suggested in particular that writing for publication differs from dissertation writing in a key way. While in writing a dissertation one tends to build an argument through providing a theoretical and empirical framework, empirical evidence and then finally stating the overall argument and findings, writing for publication requires the author to clearly state claims first, and then provide evidence to support those claims. This small piece of advice changed the way I approached my writing.

Colleagues at the University of Pittsburgh also provided critical advice when I received feedback from editors and reviewers on revising articles for resubmission. First and foremost, a senior colleague told me that receiving a 'revise and resubmit' is cause for celebration, not despair. He suggested that I set the paper aside for no more than one week before beginning to work on the revisions. He reminded me that the primary reason good papers do not get published is because authors put papers that receive 'revise and resubmits' at the bottom of a drawer and never return to the revisions.

As I began to approach my first set of revisions, I learned that the hardest part about writing for publication is not constructing an initial draft, but instead it is making revisions that keep with the integrity of the manuscript while also addressing the challenges of the reviewers and editors. A third colleague at the University of Pittsburgh helped me to balance these competing goals by teaching me to carefully 'translate' the editor's decision letter and to write persuasive arguments in my letter responding to the editor and reviewers. For instance, in one paper I wrote, all three of the reviewers asked me to provide a number of additional sources to support one of my theoretical frames. However, the editor wrote, 'I must say that I thought your rendering of the issue was rather nuanced and I worry that further discussion will only belabour and perhaps confuse rather than illuminate [your point].' Therefore, my colleague suggested that I read the reviewers' suggestions on this issue carefully, taking their advice where I felt it appropriate, but remembering that the editor suggested that he did not necessarily agree with the reviewers. In my revised draft I did make a few minor changes to this section and wrote the following in my letter to the editor, 'All three reviewers suggested that I add additional references; however, the editors suggested that further discussion might confuse rather than illuminate the issue. In considering both of these concerns I added one additional paragraph that acknowledges significant and seminal work that has been conducted by authors such as . . .' In sum, I learned that carefully crafting a response letter can be just as important as making the requested revisions.

All of this suggests that doctoral students/assistant professors benefit from mentoring by more than one faculty member. One survey of 19 doctoral students and 27 assistant professors (Cobb *et al.*, 2006) found that relying on one single mentor can be problematic, particularly when this mentoring is not helpful. In contrast to the model of single, assigned mentors, students may benefit more from having a number of mentors, as well as being encouraged to seek out informal contacts at conferences or through establishing online professional learning networks.

Further, doctoral students/assistant professors also benefit from mentoring from their peers; for example, students who are at the end of the dissertation writing process providing feedback to those just beginning the process in peer-feedback writing groups (Lee and Boud, 2003). Amanda participated in a peer-feedback group during the last three years of her doctoral programme:

During my second year in graduate school, three other women and I formed what we called a 'dissertation support group'. Only one of us was even close to writing a dissertation when we formed the group, but our goal was to support one another as we developed and negotiated topics with our advisors, wrote our dissertation proposal, and constructed empirical and theoretical reviews of literature. I was a member of the group at the earliest stage in my program and found it very beneficial to talk with people who were ahead of me in the process. My three peers often read papers I wrote for classes, giving me advice on how better to craft arguments and on theoretical, empirical, and methodological frameworks that might aid me in making claims. And, I learned that even as a very junior scholar, I had important feedback to offer my peers.

While a primary goal of our support group was to help one another in our writing, another goal was to help one another learn how to navigate the world of academia as women. Given that men still outnumber women in many fields, and given the unique challenges of planning families while balancing active roles as an academics, we felt we needed all the support we could get. Ultimately, the four of us emerged from this process with four PhDs, one divorce, two marriages, and two babies. What I gained personally from this group was confidence and proficiency in speaking professionally with my peers about my work.

Conclusions

Cultural-historical activity theory (CHAT) provides a useful framework for considering how institutional forces create competing demands and for understanding what motivates people as they engage in activities within particular communities (Engeström, 1987; Russell, 1997; Russell and Yanez, 2003). In this chapter we have employed a CHAT framework in order to consider both the competing activity systems and demands that students encounter in the course of doctoral studies and several mentoring activities that are effective for helping students to negotiate these competing demands and to develop cohesive academic identities and critical tools for becoming published scholars as they enter academic positions outside graduate school.

In this chapter we highlighted three activity systems that students encounter in doctoral studies – systems related to teaching, dissertation writing and the academic job search. On the surface, these systems may seem coherent and aligned. However, upon closer examination, they often have competing outcomes and goals. For instance, doctoral students often spend a great deal of time and energy on teaching – developing new courses, researching unfamiliar topics, and reading articles and books to prepare the best texts for a course. Although these can be necessary steps in reaching the goal of becoming a successful university-level teacher, they can also compete with the goals of dissertation writing, which are to spend time thoroughly investigating and writing about a key issue in current scholarly discourse. Likewise, it seems logical that writing a dissertation would align well with searching for an academic job. However, the goals of these systems can also compete. For instance, the goal of writing a dissertation is typically to construct a five-chapter text detailing an empirical study that will be acceptable for the requirements of a PhD. The goals of those looking to hire a doctoral candidate as a new assistant professor are somewhat different. Typically, hiring committees are looking for candidates who have not only completed the requirements of the dissertation, but also established scholarly identities and lines of publishable, current research.

Drawing from our own experiences as doctoral student and mentor, we pointed in this chapter to four key mentoring strategies that helped Amanda in negotiating the competing demands of the activity systems of doctoral studies and ultimately assisted her in developing an identity as a published scholar. By engaging in collaborative research with Amanda, Richard modelled for Amanda how to incorporate elements of their research into teaching, thereby better aligning teaching and research in their goals and outcomes. This collaborative research also served as a space for Amanda to adopt some of Richard's scholarly dispositions, while concurrently developing her own identity and agenda, thereby leading her to a dissertation topic that was both current and unique. By co-publishing research with Amanda, Richard helped Amanda to acquire skills and dispositions for scholarly writing and publishing that went beyond constructing a dissertation. For instance, Amanda learned how to negotiate roles and relationships in co-writing, write for specific audiences and journals, and frame rhetorical arguments within current scholarly debates. By engaging Amanda in reciprocal review and evaluation, Richard helped Amanda to see herself as an independent scholar in her own right – someone who could critique the arguments of more established scholars and consider feedback from others in a productive rather than defensive manner. Finally, in mentoring Amanda in the nuances of professional networking, Richard taught Amanda the value of promoting her own work and developing a national identity as a scholar and a writer. Each of these mentoring strategies aided Amanda in gaining critical skills and dispositions that she continued to draw upon as she established a scholarly identity and negotiated the competing activity systems associated with her position as an assistant professor.

In sum, we argue in this chapter that effective mentoring of doctoral students to foster publication involves more than simply providing feedback to their writing. It involves the assumption that writing and publishing are collaborative, social activities. Through her experiences with Richard, Amanda acquired beliefs and practices that served to reposition her identity to being and becoming a published scholar.

Note

1 In this chapter, we refer to doctoral advisors or supervisors as mentors, realizing that others, including peers, could serve as mentors.

References

Beach, R. (2004) 'Researching Response to Literature and the Media', in A. Goodwyn and A. Stables (eds) *Learning to Read Critically in Language and Literacy*, Thousand Oaks, CA: Sage, pp. 123–48.

Beach, R., Appleman, D., Hynds, S. and Wilhelm, J. (2005) *Teaching Literature to Adolescents*, New York: Routledge.

Beach, R. and Myers, J. (2001) *Inquiry-Based Instruction: Engaging Students in Life and Literature*, New York: Teachers College Press.

Beach, R. and Thein, A. H. (2009) 'Being and Becoming an English Educator: Constructing Identities in an English Education Doctoral Program', in A. Carey-Webb (ed.) *The Doctoral Degree in English Education*, Kennesaw, GA: Kennesaw State University Press.

Beach, R., Thein, A. H. and Parks, D. (2007) *High School Students' Social World: Negotiating Identities and Allegiances through Responding to Multicultural Literature*, Mahwah, NJ: Lawrence Erlbaum Associates.

Berkenkotter, C. and Huckin, T. (1995) *Genre Knowledge in Disciplinary Communication: Cognition/Culture/Power*, Hillsdale, NJ: Lawrence Erlbaum Associates.

Berkenkotter, C. and Thein, A. H. (2005) 'Settings, Speech Genres, and the Institutional Organization of Practices,' in R. Beach, J. Green, M. Kamil and T. Shanahan (eds) *Multidisciplinary Perspectives in Literacy Research*, 2nd edn, Cresskill, NJ: Hampton Press, pp. 179–208.

Bonilla-Silva, E. (2001) *White Supremacy and Racism in the Post-Civil Rights Era*, Boulder, CO: Lynne Rienner.

Cameron, D. (2007) *The Myth of Mars and Venus: Do Men and Women Really Speak Different Languages?*, Milton Keynes: Open University Press.

Cobb, M., Fox, D. L., Many, J. E., Matthews, M. W., McGrail, E., Taylor, D. L., Wallace, F. H., and Wamg, Y. (2006) 'Mentoring in Literacy Education: A Commentary from Graduate Students, Untenured Professors, and Tenured Professors. *Mentoring and Tutoring*, 14, 371–87.

Ede, L. and Lunsford, A. (1990) *Singular Texts/Plural Authors: Perspectives on Collaborative Writing*, Carbondale: Southern Illinois University Press.

Ehrenberg, R. G., Jakubson, G. H., Groen, J. A., So, E. and Price, J. (2007) 'Inside the Black Box of Doctoral Education: What Program Characteristics Influence Doctoral Students' Attrition and Graduation Probabilities', *Education Evaluation and Policy Analysis*, 29 (2), 134–50.

Engeström, Y. (1987) *Learning by Expanding: An Activity-Theoretical Approach to Developmental Research*, Helsinki: Orienta-Konsultit.

Gardner, S. K., Hayes, M. T. and Neider, X. N. (2007) 'The Dispositions and Skills of a PhD in Education: Perspectives of Faculty and Graduate Students in One College of Education', *Innovative Higher Education*, 31, 287–99.

Gee, J. (1996) *Social Linguistics and Literacies*, 2nd edn, New York: Falmer.

Heath, T. (2002) 'A Quantitative Analysis of PhD Students' Views of Supervision', *Higher Education Research and Development*, 21 (1), 41–53.

Holligan, C. (2005) 'Fact and Fiction: A Case History of Doctoral Supervision', *Educational Research*, 47 (3), 267–78.

Kamler, B. (2008) 'Rethinking Doctoral Publication Practices: Writing from and beyond the Thesis', *Studies in Higher Education*, 33 (3), 283–94.

Kamler, B. and Thomson, P. (2006) *Helping Doctoral Students Write: Pedagogies for Supervision*, New York: Routledge.

Kamler, B. and Thomson, P. (2008) 'The Failure of Dissertation Advice Books: Toward Alternative Pedagogies for Doctoral Writing', *Educational Researcher*, 37 (8), 507–14.

Kilbourn, B. (2006) 'The Qualitative Doctoral Dissertation Proposal', *Teachers College Record*, 108 (4), 529–76.

Lee, A. and Boud, D. (2003) 'Writing Groups, Change and Academic Identity: Research Development as Local Practice', *Studies in Higher Education*, 28 (2), 187–201.

Lovitts, B. E. (2001) *Leaving the Ivory Tower*, New York: Rowman and Littlefield.

Lundell, D. and Beach, R. (2003) 'Dissertation Writers' Negotiations with Competing Activity Systems', in C. Bazerman and D. R. Russell (eds) *Writing Selves/Writ-*

ing Societies: Research from Activity Perspectives, http://wac.colostate.edu/books/selves_societies/ (accessed 7 March 2008).

Mullen, C. A. (2005) *The Mentorship Primer*, New York: Peter Lang.

Mullen, C. A. (2007) 'Trainers, Illusionists, Tricksters, and Escapists: Changing the Doctoral Circus', *Educational Forum*, 71 (4), 300–15.

Nettles, M. T. and Millett, C. M. (2006) *Three Magic Letters: Getting to PhD*, Baltimore: Johns Hopkins University Press.

Prior, P. (1994) 'Response, Revision, Disciplinarity: A Microhistory of a Dissertation Prospectus in Sociology', *Written Communication*, 11, 483–533.

Prior, P. (1998) *Writing/Disciplinarity: A Sociohistorical Account of Literate Activity in the Academy*, Mahwah, NJ: Lawrence Erlbaum Associates.

Prior, P. and Min, Y. (2008) 'The Lived Experience of Graduate Work and Writing: From Chronotopic Laminations to Everyday Lamentations', in C. P. Casanave and X. Li (eds) *Learning the Literate Practices of Graduate School: Insiders' Reflections on Academic Enculturation*, Ann Arbor: University of Michigan Press, pp. 230–46.

Russell, D. (1997) 'Rethinking Genre in School and Society: An Activity Theory Analysis', *Written Communication*, 14, 504–54.

Russell, D. and Yanez, A. (2003) 'Big Picture People Rarely Become Historians: Genre Systems and the Contradictions of General Education', in C. Bazerman and D. Russell (eds) *Writing Selves/Writing Societies*, http://wac.colostate.edu/books/selves_societies/ (accessed 7 April 2008).

Thein, A. H. (2005) *Discourses of Femininity?: Mapping the Social and Cultural Words of High School Girls through their Stances and Responses to Literature*, unpublished doctoral dissertation, University of Minnesota.

Wenger, E. (1998) *Communities of Practice: Learning, Meaning, and Identity*, New York: Cambridge University Press.

Chapter 9

Learning about journal publication

The pedagogies of editing a 'special issue'

Pat Thomson, Tina Byrom, Carol Robinson and Lisa Russell

Despite the development of, and arguments for, alternative genres of open access and devolved publication (Smith, 1999; Willinsky, 2006), writing for commercially produced scholarly journals continues to be significant. In Britain, for example, academic 'output' in the social sciences is measured and judged, in the national Research Assessment Exercise (RAE), largely on the basis of single-authored books (the scholarly monograph) and peer-refereed journal articles. The current proposal to change the RAE process to focus more strongly on citations makes the work of publishing in high-status and publicly indexed journals not simply a necessity, but a high-pressure imperative.

This chapter addresses a key, but largely neglected, aspect of this irrevocably performative textual production – how it is that doctoral and early career researchers might come to learn and understand the game of academic journal publication (Lee and Kamler, 2008). It focuses on the process of editing a journal and reports on one case, that of a special issue of the journal *Improving Schools*.

The chapter is constructed as a multi-vocal narrative. The main thread is Pat, writing as 'I'. The other three voices are those of Tina, Carol and Lisa, three researchers at various stages in their careers. They have written about their editorial experiences in response to my questions, and I edited the responses into a first draft of the chapter, which was then discussed and reworded by the whole group. The final chapter is a mutually agreed formulation, although I have retained stylistic control of the main narrative and have also written a pedagogic reflection on the process. I have retained large pieces of the writing of the three special issue editors as a means of representing their various perspectives on events. I begin by providing some background to the special issue and then report the co-editors' motivations for involvement and their experiences. The chapter concludes with some reflections on what we variously learned during and after the process.

A focus on text and identity

It was perhaps not surprising that, after a long career combining school and system leadership and management with classroom English teaching and regular practitioner publications, I became interested in the situated practices of scholarly writing. My own doctorate (Thomson, 1999) had an explicit focus on research as writing (Richardson, 1994) and experimented with a variety of written ways of conducting and representing my inquiry. This interest morphed into explicit 'writing' programmes for doctoral students and into collaborative practitioner-research studies with Barbara Kamler on the pedagogies of doctoral writing – or what we call text work/identity work (Kamler and Thomson, 2001, 2004, 2006, 2007, 2008) in recognition of the ways in which both the scholar and her scholarship are produced in texts and their performances. Our joint work has focused on the anxieties that doctoral students experience when engaging in new forms of text production. We have deliberately avoided an approach that promotes technical tips and tricks, and work instead with pedagogies that build a robustly theorized repertoire of metaphors, diagnostics, exercises and situated exemplars grounded in the realpolitik of supervision, the dissertation examination and scholarly career formation.

My own academic publishing career had begun before I entered higher education, but because of my very late entry into the academy I did feel a need to establish myself relatively quickly. I edited two special issue international journals as a deliberate strategy of foregrounding a particular issue that I saw as important but currently downplayed within the field. At the same time these special issues allowed me to stake a claim in a field of inquiry, build networks and profile, and get two good peer-reviewed publications. I am still pleased to claim on my curriculum vitae the first special issue of a journal on media and education policy (*Journal of Education Policy*, 2004, 19(3)), and the first on Bourdieu and educational leadership (*International Journal of Leadership in Education*, 2003, 6(4)). In both instances I approached the editors at conferences, assisted by introductions from existing colleagues, and then followed up with a written proposal.

Through these experiences I came to the view that editing a special issue was a helpful strategy for early career researchers. Thus, when the opportunity presented itself to move from work with doctoral and early career researchers on writing the dissertation and conference and journal papers, to editing a special issue journal, it seemed only 'natural' to pursue it.

How the special issue came to be

The special issue arose from an ESRC-funded seminar series[1] entitled 'Engaging Critically with Pupil Voice'. Pupil voice is the term used in the UK to describe activities that involve young people taking a greater role in decisions about their own education. It encompasses a range of activities, including consultation, student councils and forums, negotiated curriculum and active citizenship approaches, and students as researchers (see Cook-Sather, 2002; Fielding, 2004; Rudduck and Flutter, 2004; Thomson and Gunter, 2007). The seminar aimed to map the activities that went under the title of 'pupil voice', delineate key advances and debates, and locate gaps in the field. The series was a partnership between the Universities of Nottingham (Pat Thomson), Sussex (Michael Fielding) and Manchester Metropolitan, and a now defunct government school funding initiative, Networked Learning Communities.

A condition of ESRC funding is that seminar series have a research training function. All successful seminars must demonstrate how doctoral and early career researchers can participate, and what they are expected to learn. We made this a high priority, together with involving teachers, peak bodies of community youth organizations and young people themselves. Seminars are also expected to translate into scholarly outputs, and every one of our six seminars discussed the kinds of publications that might result. We eventually decided to pursue an edited book, *Doing Visual Research with Children and Young People* (Thomson, 2008), and two special journal issues, *Discourse* (2007) 28(3), edited by Michael Fielding, and *Improving Schools* (2007) 10(1), edited by Tina Byrom, Carol Robinson and Lisa Russell. There were also individual journal articles written by seminar participants and submitted to other publications (e.g. Bragg, 2007; Cook-Sather and Youens, 2007; Cruddas, 2007).

I had suggested these two journals because pupil voice 'fitted' their foci: *Discourse* was an appropriate outlet for articles that took up theoretical debates, whereas *Improving Schools* has, as its prime goal, changing schools according to principles of social justice. It is also important to note that I know the editors of both journals and am on the editorial board of *Improving Schools*: Terry Wrigley, the editor, was/is enthusiastic about giving editorial experience to early career researchers. I did the initial negotiations about both special issues and Michael produced a formal proposal for consideration by the *Discourse* editorial board.

The editorial opportunities for early career researchers thus arose, as did my own earlier editing experience, through the networks of more experienced scholars. Networks also determined which early career researchers were to have those opportunities: in this case it was decided through nominations from Michael and Pat. The editorial team was to consist of four people: two early career researchers and two doctoral students nearing completion. Carol Robinson had worked with Michael on projects, and a second proposed editor was competing her doctorate at Sussex under Michael's supervision; Lisa Russell was working as a researcher with me (Thomson and Russell, 2007) and I also co-supervised Tina Byrom's doctoral research. It was indeed a case of 'who you know' as it so often is in academia – as elsewhere. (I revisit academic networks in the conclusion to the chapter, together with mentoring and patronage.) Contributions were to come from presentations made during the seminars; the possible contributions were finalized at the last seminar meeting, but it was made clear that all content would be subject to a peer-refereeing process. Thus, the inexperienced editors did not have to solicit content. Rather, their task was to manage the process through which those people who wished to contribute could achieve this goal. Michael and I were to provide support if and when necessary.

It is important to the narrative to note the ways in which I thought about the process of 'support' at this time.

The editorial zone

Through our work on academic writing Barbara Kamler and I have continued to wrestle with the permutations of the apprenticeship approach to doctoral supervision/advising. We have argued that it metaphorically and materially assumes a one-way transmission of knowledge, downplays the kinds of knowledges and experiences that doctoral researchers bring to their research and assumes a kind of infallibility in supervisors/advisers that seldom exists. This approach is born in part from our own experiences of moving from the school sector into higher education, but it also comes from immersion in debates about practitioner research and professional doctorates (Anderson and Herr, 1999; Cochran-Smith and Lytle, 1999; Green, Maxwell and Shanahan, 2001) and our conversations with doctoral researchers in courses and workshops.

My approach to the special issue was rooted in this critique. It was the intention of me and/or Michael not to act as editor with the four seminar participants as our apprentices, but rather to create a situation where they could learn from each other as they tackled the various tasks involved in editorial work. This was an inchoate Vygotskian approach: it assumed a zone of proximal development or ZPD – 'a distance between the actual developmental level . . . and the potential development as determined through problem solving . . . in collaboration with more capable peers' (Vygotsky, 1978: 86). I assumed that the editorial tasks created an order for collective learning and that there was no need for me to make explicit the kinds of editorial understandings that might be constructed, and the skills that might be required. This approach was born from the conviction that these were capable adults with existing knowledges about journals and academic writing and publishing who did not need to be spoon-fed or to act as editorial assistants to an experienced editorial chief.

Subsequent to the issue being produced, and provoked by the writing of this chapter, I have decided that some scaffolding might indeed have been useful. I explain this in the conclusion.

Editing *Improving Schools*: the editors' stories

Reasons for involvement

Carol: I viewed it as a challenge. I'd not previously been involved in any similar work, although I had played a significant role in the writing of two books, several research reports and some peer-reviewed published articles. I was aware of the review process and was excited about experiencing the process as an editor. Most of my writing had been done with at least one other academic and, although I had led the writing on some of the papers, I had been sole author for only one paper and lacked confidence in my ability to write without input from others. I also lacked confidence to write anything too controversial, although I would happily challenge ideas during discussions.

I enjoy working as a team and was looking forward to working with the other co-editors. The fact that none of us had previous experience of editing was, to me, an advantage as it meant that I was likely to have the opportunity to play a major role in all aspects of the process. I felt a sense of confidence as there were two key people, Pat T. and Michael F., who could be called upon if the need arose. In addition, I was safe in the knowledge that Michael F. wouldn't have approached me about being one of the co-editors if he wasn't sure that I could contribute positively to the editorial team.

I am passionate about 'pupil voice' and saw the potential for work in this area to be published – and to have my name associated with it was even better.

Lisa: There are a number of reasons why I agreed to do this. I enjoy new challenges and I saw value in putting in the extra work required to get this special edition together. Being in the early stages of my career I was enthusiastic to learn more about 'pupil voice' and I believed I had something to contribute. I was keen to expand my research and writing profile and saw this as an opportunity that would enhance my knowledge about the editing process, enable me to gain more publications and develop my academic skills. Furthermore, I had a strong support network. I knew one member of the team (Tina) very well and knew I could successfully work with her. I saw merit in working with another university and I believed this would help the editing process and improve my cross-university links. I was safe in the knowledge that we all had similar research interests and philosophies because we'd all attended the same seminar series. I also knew we had the support and guidance of my line manager should we need it. So, although I felt I was engaging in unknown territories, I also knew I was working with a strong team that could help me make a success of this task.

At the time I was still trying to find my writer identity and explore what it was I could write and why. I had four publications and had reviewed a couple of papers for two other journals. After writing my PhD I didn't particularly enjoy the task of writing, preferring instead to be out in the field and gathering the data. Consequently many of my earlier publications focused on the research process/methodology, as this was something I felt I was good at, I understood and could write in confidence about.

Tina: At the beginning of the co-editing process I was a final-year PhD student struggling to write a thesis. I had some previous experience of working on a funded project with Pat but didn't feel that this provided me with any directly relevant experience upon which to draw during the co-editing process. I was of course happy to have been asked, but also felt quite uncertain whether I was up to the task. When initial conversations with Pat had alluded to my involvement in co-editing the journal I was a little surprised. I didn't feel that my performance as a PhD student warranted the level of trust that came with co-editing a journal. I agreed to do it, partly because Pat had approached me to do it, but also because I knew that it would look good in terms of my research profile. I was also looking forward to working with others from both the University of Nottingham and the University of Sussex.

I hoped that I would learn more about getting published and the whole process of publishing in an academic journal. At the beginning of the process I knew very little about publishing, but did have some vague ideas of how to go about it based on hearsay more than direct experience or concrete information. I particularly wanted to use this experience as a stepping-stone into the world of academic writing and publishing and therefore approached it with enthusiasm.

What actually happened and what was learned

Carol: The reality of being one of the co-editors kicked in at the final ESRC seminar when the editorial team met to discuss the publisher's deadlines for receiving the articles, proofreading and publication. We planned a timeline of events; it was at this stage that we realized that we were up against a tight schedule and allocated various tasks to the two different university teams (Sussex and Nottingham). I expected that members of each team would work together to ensure all tasks were complete by the deadlines we or the publishers had set. The two teams took joint responsibility for contacting possible authors asking whether they intended submitting papers. The Sussex team then took responsibility for contacting possible peer reviewers, and in due course for distributing submitted papers to them. In reality this meant that I did all of this work, largely as time was of the essence and I knew that, if I took responsibility for this aspect of the editing process, it would get done within the limited time scale.

From the initial meeting at the end of the seminar series until the publication of the journal, literally hundreds of emails were sent between the editorial team, updating each other on progress being made, and asking many questions, ranging from, in some cases, relatively small issues such as the wording of emails to the publisher or potential authors, to more significant issues such as the ordering of papers for the journal and discussions about which papers to include and which to exclude.

During the editing process several tasks emerged that we had not planned for. In most instances these needed completing within a short time scale, for example deciding on the order of the articles, writing the editorial, writing the book reviews and selecting the 'pupil voice' comments for the front cover of the journal.

Tina: Although we assigned referees to each paper, the co-editing team also read through submitted articles. This helped focus our thoughts on the editorial that needed to be written. We felt that it was important to have an overview of all the papers that were coming in to get a sense of the different perspectives that were emerging around the whole notion of pupil voice.

During the process it became clear that we had to recruit more referees. I called upon other academics at the University of Nottingham, who gladly stepped in to review articles at quite short notice. I enjoyed having to do this as it provided me with opportunities to claim some ground in the development of an academic identity: it was almost as though my involvement with the process was providing me with increased credibility amongst my peers.

Numerous emails were passed around the team; emails centred on the quality of the papers and discussions about how we would justify the exclusion of some papers. I was surprised by the quality of some of the submissions, which I considered, even in my novice state, as pretty poor! This gave me increased confidence that, although I found writing articles quite tricky, I did have an intuitive feel for what made a good article. This did raise some tensions when having to detail the limitations of other people's work, particularly after having spent so much time with the authors during the seminar series. I was actually quite lily-livered in this and asked Carol to inform people that their articles had not been accepted for publication.

Lisa: Tina and I met on a regular basis to discuss our progress and issues; this was easier given that we were located at the same university, we very much worked as a team and often contacted the other two editors after our meeting, during which we would agree on the content of emails and/ or telephone conversations with authors. After the initial meeting three of us met only once face-to-face at a BERA conference. In hindsight I think it would have been beneficial for us all to have met face-to-face more regularly. We each worked out our roles mostly by offering our own services for tasks we felt we were capable of and indeed wanted to do. It was a very proactive management approach.

The process almost led itself in the sense that we each volunteered to do set tasks as they came tumbling upon us. At points we were unsure about whether we were fulfilling everything we needed to be. We used Pat to check that we weren't missing anything major and to confirm our choice of papers. She also helped with the resubmission points outlined for papers we needed to resubmit after amendments.

Initially I hadn't thought about the book reviews and didn't quite know how to go about doing one. After talking with the other editors and Pat we decided to ask publishers about giving us suggestions at their stands at BERA. Here contacts with publishers commenced and relevant book titles revealed themselves. After reading other book reviews and the book I was going to review I set to writing about it. We each checked each other's writing sections and offered comments for improvement for one another. There were a number of other unexpected issues that arose from the editing process, mainly the shock about the amount of time and effort it took. Chasing authors took a lot longer than expected. Responding to authors was trickier than I first expected. Particularizing the careful detail and tone of encouragement and support for them to improve the paper, especially when some authors were well known, was difficult. I sometimes felt a little unsure about questioning some authors and their work/writing abilities, but had to find the confidence to do this to push for better papers. I'm not sure how I would have coped having to go through this process on my own, as I found the general email, telephone and face-to-face contact invaluable in helping me assert my ideas and confidence in moving forward.

Tina: There were things that came in at the end which required a quick response and I found that I was communicating with Kathy Westwood, the liaison editor at Sage, more frequently and without consulting with the rest of the team. I think there were some times when decisions had to be made, and when I couldn't get hold of Lisa or Carol I just had to make them. I found this slightly uncomfortable as it went against how we had worked throughout the entire process. For example, after the team had agreed on the sentences that were to appear on the front cover, Kathy informed me that they had to be shorter and more 'snappy'. As Kathy needed them to be changed almost by return of email, I just had to get on and do it – I hoped that the other team members would like them, but it felt quite risky to be doing that and it didn't feel right.

Later on in the process I found myself in a position where I was chasing up consent forms from authors. I found this particularly frustrating when a particular author had not returned their form and was also not responding to emails about it. I can remember feeling particularly cross when the form eventually arrived by email via an administrator rather than the author: I took this as a marker of hierarchy and that I was clearly not as important as the author. However, on reflection it was probably more to do with the very real time constraints that academics have to work under!

I also found myself proofreading the articles when they came through from Sage. I can't quite remember how this happened, but I think they came through at a busy time before the Christmas break and had to be back with Sage quite promptly.

Such things made the end of the process feel quite rushed and frantic.

Reflections on the editing experience

In this section I reflect first of all on some of the emotional dimensions of the editorial process and then go on to consider the pedagogical.

The emotional dimensions of the special issue

The social-relational dimensions of the editing experience were not only significant, but also as important as the more intellectual aspects of editing in which the three early career researchers were embedded.

The importance of the offer of collegiality, a contrast to the somewhat solitary pursuits of both the doctoral researcher (Tina) and the lone field-worker (Lisa), is apparent in the editors' narratives. Being able to learn something new, in the company of like others, provided a kind of safety net against the possibility of making a drastic mistake. And being approached and/or invited by a senior academic who also offered some, albeit remote, support was also key. This signified confidence in emergent scholarly abilities. Acceptance of the invitation also had an element of compliance to the wishes of scholars who could have direct influence on career trajectories through offers of employment and writing of references. I suspect that there may be something gendered in this response and it may well be that some younger, ambitious male researchers do not feel the same kinds of uncertainties and tentativeness as were felt here.

However, these affective dimensions were impacted by the group's experiences of two very difficult issues. Most special issue editors manage to get through the one-off process without having to deal with anything but routine editing, whereas permanent editors do encounter potentially tricky events relatively regularly. Tina, Carol and Lisa did have to deal with much more than they – and indeed Michael and I – had bargained for.

The first issue concerned a particular article written by young adults who had taken a very active part in the seminar series. The editors had all been particularly keen to have their thoughts included in the special issue. *Improving Schools* had a tradition of printing narratives of good practice, not refereeing them and putting them in a section called 'accounts of practice' so it was clear that this was what they were. The editors thought that this would allow the young people more freedom to write what and how they wanted. However, when the article came in, it was clear it needed a lot more work to be made publishable, and the editors had to make a decision about what to do. After much soul searching among the group, I edited and partly rewrote the piece, which was then returned to the authors for approval. After they did some further minor adjustments, the editors thought the matter was resolved and it was scheduled for publication. But at the very last minute there was another crisis. In Tina's words:

> I struggled to contact one of the authors of the paper and had to chase this up via the organization within which they had been working at the time of writing. During the time we were editing, the management of the institution had changed and they refused to allow the paper to go to publication as it stood. There were numerous political reasons as to why this was the case, but it went against the remit of the publication to exclude this particular paper. I had to consult with both Pat and Sage on this issue.

In the end the paper was omitted because, according to English law, there had to be a signed permission in order to publish. Nevertheless all of us saw the actions of the organization as a clear case of censorship of young people's opinions. Acting according to the legalities of the commercial publishing world on which we were dependent thus went directly against our philosophical/political purposes and commitments.

The second issue was troubling and painful, and there are significant ethical difficulties in discussing it in print. At the outset of this chapter I reported that there were originally four editors, and yet it is clear from the narratives of the process that there are only three. This is because towards the end of the editing process it became obvious that there was a difference of view around what counted as teamwork, who did what and when, and who ought to be credited as editors. It is fair to say that this generated a great deal of discussion, some sleepless nights, reflections about how the process might have been better organized and a lot of varying emotions. The end result was a decision by three of the group to claim editorship. The discussion of how this happened and what to say in public continued from the editorial process into the writing of this chapter. We collectively decided in the end that a small comment was necessary but sufficient. These kinds of incidents are part and parcel of academic life, in which collegiality occurs against/ within a competitive environment and scholarly identities can be both made and undone through teamwork. The editors and I hope that readers of this chapter will interpret the bald description of the problem and solution given here, and imagine some of the kinds of time-consuming and demanding events and discussions that occurred. As a result of this experience, the editors now agree on the importance of negotiating roles and responsibilities at the outset of any collective process, anticipating potential problems and making explicit a set of protocols for handling any that arise.

Reflections on editing as a social discursive practice

As I have reflected on the kinds of processes that the editors experienced I have begun to develop a set of categories that might begin to serve as the basis for editing pedagogies. It is important to note that this is work that is beginning rather than being fully fledged.

The written accounts of the experiences of the three editors make it clear that the experience did have significant positive aspects. Their narratives show that they engaged in philosophical work, through writing an editorial and choosing books for review; market work, through negotiations with the publisher, although this was not spread evenly around the group; profile work, through the activities that enhanced their own scholarly careers, networks and identities; relational work, through working with each other, with referees and with authors; textual work, through selection of articles and giving feedback to authors; and secretarial work through the process of refereeing and production. I elaborate these categories a little later in this section and marry them to an understanding of journal editing as the publication, production and interpretation of texts following the particular conventions of academic peer review – a discursive and social practice (see Kamler and Thomson, 2006: 20–3). Wellington (2003: 75) notes that editors describe their role as 'enhancers, improvers, disseminators, shapers, of a field, mentors and mediators'. I agree but suggest that journal editing might be further understood as interrelated layers of activity in which the middle layer is the editors' *mediation* of authors' texts, according to these categories of activity (see Figure 9.1, a further working of Kamler and Thomson, 2006: 21).

The kinds of editorial mediations that are made – and are possible – are strongly framed by both academic and commercial publishing constraints, expectations and customs. Many of these are taken for granted and inexplicit. Academics come to know the 'rules' of writing journal articles simply by being in and playing the game, getting it wrong (having publications rejected), being told by mentors what is expected, reading advice and other books on academic publishing, and/or analysing texts for themselves. Because editing journals is a more narrowly distributed pursuit, scholars find that, whereas they might know about the scholarly conventions that operate around journal publication, they know little of the commercial aspects of scholarly publication until they are a member of an editorial board, or an editor of a special issue. It is thus helpful to elaborate the heuristic of mediating practices further.

The kinds of mediating actions that are accepted as 'fitting' editing practice, and thus befit an editor, are numerous and include the six below.

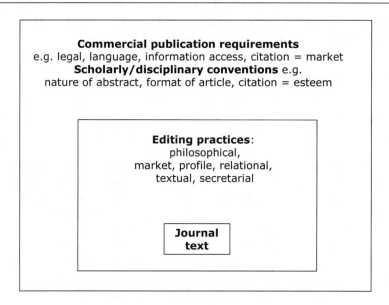

Figure 9.1 The discursive production of a journal text.

Philosophical/ideological work

Editors must determine the purposes of publishing particular kinds of texts. They do so through writing and rewriting the overall mission of the journal and regular editorials, constructing referee forms and representing the journal in meetings and conferences. Editors of journal special issues need to show how their intents match and enhance those of the journal.

Market work

Editors are committed to establishing a readership. In commercially published journals this involves them, and editorial boards, in discussions with publishers about and activities geared towards getting market share through subscriptions, downloads, citations and positions in citation league tables. Market considerations influence the approval of special issues. If special issue editors can show that there may be new readers attracted through specific marketing strategies, this enhances their proposal.

Profile work

The editorship of journals brings institutional prestige as well as individual curriculum vitae advantages. Journal editorship is a marker of reputation, peer esteem and accomplishment. Journal editors also seek to enhance the esteem of the publication and its individual/institutional affiliates through building up a prestigious editorial board and a notable and authoritative set of referees. Editorship of special issues can be an important step for individual scholars as they seek to build their networks and standing in the field.

Relational work

Editing requires interaction and negotiation with the academic and professional community. Differences of opinion can easily become conflicts because much more is at stake than publication. Egos and emotions, but also identities and reputations, are constructed through the submission and refereeing processes. Similar complexities are embedded in collaborative work with colleagues on the editorial team and board. Editors of special issues must manage this work with the same tact and effect as permanent editors.

Textual work

Editors have the ultimate responsibility for ensuring that articles are of good quality, that is, they have an argument that is well written, conforms to conventions and makes a contribution to knowledge. Editors set referee frameworks that will assist in this process, develop templates for abstracts and write guidelines for submission that attempt to make clear to authors what they expect. They must also manipulate referee comments into a set of comprehensible recommendations for writers or into encouragement to resubmit. They must write positive and constructive letters of rejection. Special issue editors must maintain quality by managing the refereeing tasks efficiently and effectively, avoiding any complaints going to the permanent editor or the publisher.

Secretarial work

Although not necessarily doing all of this work themselves, editors must ensure that they meet the time-pressured mechanics of getting the refereeing done, the articles finalized, putting together the issue, writing the editorial, and getting the text to the publisher. They must ensure that the articles have abstracts and key words that allow them to be digitally searched. They must ensure they are written in correct and appropriate English – and English is now increasingly dominant in academic publication (Mandal, 2000). Finally they have to follow up any legal requirements, including unsigned permission forms. Special issue editors often do not have editorial assistance available to them and must do these tasks themselves.

It is important to reiterate that the heuristic is based on my reflection on the case in point, rather than being notions generated before the process began. This way of thinking about journal editing is complementary to texts that provide strategies for writing journal articles and getting published (Murray, 2005). I now continue in this vein, offering further reflections on how the notion of editing work as a social and discursive practice of mediation of texts might become pedagogical.

Towards editing pedagogies

As anticipated, the special issue created a learning time-space in which existing knowledges about academic publishing were able to be pooled and shared, a Vygotskian ZPD. The editing tasks created opportunities for new knowledges to be constructed and the informal practice of building 'know-how' (Schatzki, 2001). The presence of mentors and a helpful publisher on call also provided support when the group felt it was needed. This was not a 'sink or swim' experience and the group is not certain that they would have appreciated anything more formal.

But, on reflection, it seems to me that it is also possible that the editing learning might have been enhanced if there had been more formal pedagogical scaffolding provided. If it had been in existence, I might have used the heuristic of editorial work elaborated above as a stimulus for discussion. This might also have focused thinking on what could be expected and what needed to be done, while providing a metalanguage for the editors to use to critically analyse their own processes and events as they occurred. But, in the kind of case described in this chapter, such an approach would struggle to avoid (re)casting the editorial team as apprentices, working to the instructions of a more knowing expert. A more direct pedagogical approach that mobilized the categories of editing practice might be appropriate for and better suited to workshops, in which volunteers sign up for discussion about an anticipated experience. In the kind of instance reported here, when there are real editors and an actual journal, it is possible that reading an editorial case narrative would be of more interest and use. I have been unable to locate anything like this in the doctoral education literatures so far, or in my reading of the doctoral advice books. It is as if building a scholarly career stops and starts with writing journal articles and perhaps turning the thesis into a scholarly monograph. The work of editing – and indeed also refereeing – is largely missing from the litany of steps that one might take to become an employed scholar. Carol, Lisa, Tina and I hope that this chapter might be used as a narrative to stimulate the thinking of other new editors about what does and might happen.

But I do suspect that, in our case discussed here, a greater focus on text work would have been helpful. The editors were relatively confident that they could tell what was a good article and what wasn't, and did not feel the need to seek advice. Nevertheless, perhaps textual know-how could have been heightened further if I had organized a formal discussion about what counted as a 'good article'. I would certainly have learnt something from such a process and the heuristic developed so far could be complemented by a set of working criteria about what does or doesn't count as a 'good article' in a specific journal for a specific audience. Both Wellington (2003) and Yates (2004: 103), for example, address the question of 'poor quality' and rejection, with Yates summarizing that 'good' in journal terms means:

> research that addresses the agenda of that journal, takes account of what has gone before, and is seen to add to it. The quality of the methodology, contribution and writing will be in ratio to the degree of other researchers trying to publish in that journal. The article abstract extracts key selling points of methodology, focus and findings/contribution for that journal audience. The article itself cites names recognizable to and appearing elsewhere in issues of that journal. Signs that the author is a student or a newcomer are avoided.

Such a statement might be a very good beginning for an editorial discussion. Working with such an explicit set of normative rules is something I will try next time I support a group of early career researchers to edit a special issue, as well as using this narrative and thus the heuristic.

I want to conclude by reflecting briefly on the systemic cultures that legitimized giving early career researchers the experience of editing.

The emphasis by the ESRC on research training for early career and doctoral researchers was a helpful focus for the more experienced scholars in the group. It provided reasons for us to ask what we could do that would be helpful to the less academically experienced members of the team. A sympathetic journal editor and publisher were also critical for the special issue with its new editors. As I noted at the outset of the chapter, this was 'found' and negotiated through the academic networks of the senior researchers in the seminar.

I also noted earlier that the editors, Carol, Tina and Lisa, were nominated by senior researchers and they were scholars with whom Michael Fielding and I were connected, and for whom we were in some way responsible. Such mentoring is of course what senior academics are meant to do. It is written into our job descriptions and is indeed what the notion of 'professing' means – to advocate for scholarship and to encourage it in others. Yet I am very aware that this kind of support is variously distributed amongst early career and doctoral researchers. At its very worst senior colleagues can exercise patronage for the few at the expense of the many. Although individuals such as Carol, Lisa and Tina can and do benefit from editorial and other scholarly experiences made available to them as part of their career development, there is as yet not the kind of emphasis on the range of learning experiences of importance in the formation of scholars that would make equity of access and participation in them an issue. I do wonder in idle moments what kind of university cultures/structures would be able to make editing and publishing an integral part of the scholarly formation of all researchers. And, with an eye on my own workload, I know that the answer must be systemic and systematic rather than being an 'initiative' that relies on the efforts of a few individuals.

The work of journal editing

In conclusion I return to the three editors for the reasons why such systemic change would be worthwhile.

What we learned about publishing

Lisa: I found the whole process invaluable. It gave me insight and confidence in my own writing skills and ability to edit and review abstracts and manuscripts. I feel as though this task has helped enhance my CV and has given me additional credibility contributing to my academic profile.

Tina: I found working with the publisher extremely positive and would welcome the opportunity to do so again. I found the process of writing my own paper a huge challenge and was pleased to have finally achieved this. I'm not convinced that we would have done anything differently, because we weren't operating by any set rules or protocols. It felt really good to have been trusted with the role and I was extremely proud when the hard copy came through the post. All the issues and tensions that had arisen during the process seemed to mysteriously melt away at that point! I came to view myself differently as an academic. I learnt about my own potential contributions to the academic world and grew in confidence about my abilities to assess the work of others. I have placed this on my CV and did refer to it during recent interviews. I felt quite proud of what I had achieved until I realized that the people who were interviewing me had a huge publishing record and that my dabbling in that arena was, by comparison, still quite small.

Carol: The whole process was a huge learning curve. In particular, I have questioned the expectations I automatically placed on members of the team, in terms of expecting them to be active team players. I have also gained knowledge of the finer details of editing a journal and the processes involved, including handling sensitive issues when dealing with authors whose papers are not going to be accepted for publication. As a result of dealing with the reviewers, I was able to build links with many people who until then were merely names and faces. However, the email and, on occasions, telephone contact helped to build closer links with many other academics interested in the area of pupil voice.

I have benefited hugely from being involved in the editing of the journal, both for the learning that took place during the editing process and to have my name associated with the journal. I have included my involvement on my CV and as one of my RAE esteem indicators. I now hold a position as a Senior Research Fellow and consider that my role as co-editor added to my credibility as an academic and was a contributory factor (amongst many others) in me gaining a more senior research role.

Postscript

Just as we were finalizing this chapter, a further development occurred that reinforced the benefits of editorial work for scholarly career formation.

Tina: One of the main issues facing early career researchers is how to raise their profile in the academic world. One route is through networking and I have found this to be extremely valuable. Following discussions with a friend and colleague interested in a similar research area to my own, who had herself been prompted by Pat, I approached Terry Wrigley at *Improving Schools* to see whether he would consider the possibility of my co-editing another special issue, this time on participation. I didn't know how the idea would be received and felt slightly anxious that he wouldn't be interested. I was relieved and pleased when he confirmed his interest and was highly supportive of the idea, suggesting some areas that we could potentially cover within the issue. I am looking forward to co-editing the special edition and have already begun the process differently – agreeing in advance who will be responsible for particular tasks. In addition, Terry invited me onto the editorial board of *Improving Schools*, which I willingly accepted. I felt quite flattered to be asked even though some of the doubts about my capacity to do a good job resurfaced. It would seem that the journey of gaining an academic identity is not linear and is instead a highly complex process that brings many fears and anxieties.

Note

1 The seminar series archives can be found on http://www.pupil-voice.org.uk. Networked Learning Communities also has an archive on http://www.ncsl.org.uk/networked-index.htm

References

Anderson, G. and Herr, K. (1999) 'The New Paradigm Wars: Is There Room for Rigorous Practitioner Knowledge in Schools and Universities?', *Educational Researcher*, 8 (5), 12–21.

Bragg, S. (2007) ' "But I Listen to Children Anyway" – Teacher Perspectives on Pupil Voice', *Educational Action Research*, 15 (4), 505–18.

Cochran-Smith, M. and Lytle, S. (1999) 'The Teacher Research Movement: A Decade Later', *Educational Researcher*, 28 (7), 15–25.

Cook-Sather, A. (2002) 'Authorizing Students' Perspectives: Toward Trust, Dialogue, and Change in Education', *Educational Researcher*, 31 (4), 3–14.

Cook-Sather, A. and Youens, B. (2007) 'Repositioning Students in Initial Teacher Preparation: A Comparative Case Study of Learning to Teach for Social Justice in the United States and in England', *Journal of Teacher Education*, 58 (1), 62–75.

Cruddas, L. (2007) 'Engaged Voices – Dialogic Interaction and the construction of Shared Social Messages', *Educational Action Research*, 15 (3), 479–88.

Fielding, M. (2004) 'Transformative Approaches to Student Voice: Theoretical Underpinnings, Recalcitrant Realities', *British Educational Research Journal*, 30 (2), 295–311.

Green, B., Maxwell, T. and Shanahan, P. (eds) (2001) *Doctoral Education and Professional Practice: The Next Generation?*, Armidale, New South Wales: Kardoorair Press.

Kamler, B. and Thomson, P. (2001) 'Talking Down Writing Up, or, Ten Emails Make a Conference Paper', Paper presented at the Australian Association for Research in Education, Notre Dame University, Fremantle, 1–5 December.

Kamler, B. and Thomson, P. (2004) 'Driven to Abstraction: Doctoral Supervision and Writing Pedagogies', *Teaching in Higher Education*, 9 (2), 195–209.

Kamler, B. and Thomson, P. (2006) *Helping Doctoral Students Write: Pedagogies for Supervision*, London: Routledge.

Kamler, B. and Thomson, P. (2007) 'Rethinking Doctoral Work as Text Work and Identity Work', in B. Somekh and T. Schwandt (eds) *Knowledge Production: Research in Interesting Times*, London: Routledge, pp. 166–79.

Kamler, B. and Thomson, P. (2008) 'The Failure of Dissertation Advice Books: Towards Alternative Pedagogies for Doctoral Writing', *Educational Researcher*, 37 (8), 507–18.

Lee, A. and Kamler, B. (2008) 'Bringing Pedagogy to Doctoral Publishing', *Teaching in Higher Education*, 13 (5), 511–23.

Mandal, S. (2000) 'Reconsidering Cultural Globalisation: The English Language in Malaysia', *Third World Quarterly*, 21 (6), 1001–12.

Murray, R. (2005) *Writing for Academic Journals*, Buckingham: Open University Press.

Richardson, L. (1994) 'Writing: A Method of Inquiry', in N. Denzin and Y. Lincoln (eds) *The Handbook of Qualitative Research*, Thousand Oaks, CA: Sage Publications, pp. 516–29.

Rudduck, J. and Flutter, J. (2004) *How to Improve Your School*, London: Continuum.

Schatzki, T. (2001) 'Practice Mind-ed Orders', in T. Schatzki, K. Knorr and K. K. Cetina (eds) *The Practice Turn in Contemporary Theory*, London: Routledge, pp. 42–55.

Smith, J. W. (1999) 'The Deconstructed Journal – a New Model for Academic Publishing', *Learned Publishing*, 12 (2), 79–91.

Thomson, P. (1999) *Doing Justice: Stories of Everyday Life in Disadvantaged Schools and Neighbourhoods*. Unpublished PhD, Deakin University. Accessible through the Australian Digital Thesis programme, Geelong.

Thomson, P. (ed.) (2008) *Doing Visual Research with Children and Young People*, London: Routledge.

Thomson, P. and Gunter, H. (2007) 'The Methodology of Students-as-Researchers: Valuing and Using Experience and Expertise to Develop Methods', *Discourse*, 28 (3), 327–42.

Thomson, P. and Russell, L. (2007) *Mapping the Provision of Alternatives to School Exclusion*, York: Joseph Rowntree Foundation.

Vygotsky, L. (1978) *Mind in Society: The Development of Higher Psychological Processes*, Cambridge, MA: Harvard University Press.

Wellington, J. (2003) *Getting Published: A Guide for Lecturers and Researchers*, London: RoutledgeFalmer.

Willinsky, J. (2006) *The Access Principle: The Case for Open Access to Research and Scholarship*, Cambridge, MA: Massachusetts Institute of Technology.

Yates, L. (2004) *What Does Good Educational Research Look Like?*, Buckingham: Open University Press.

Index